Generations
Generations
Generations

The Story of a Church and a Movement

Billy Kennedy

with Ralph Turner

malcolm down
PUBLISHING

Copyright © Billy Kennedy and Ralph Turner 2025
First published 2025 by Malcolm Down Publishing Ltd.
www.malcolmdown.co.uk

29 28 27 26 25   7 6 5 4 3 2 1

The right of Billy Kennedy and Ralph Turner to be identified as the authors of this work has been asserted by them in accordance with the Copyright, Designs and Patents Act 1988.

All rights reserved. No part of this publication may be reproduced, stored in a retrieval system, or transmitted in any other form or by any means, electronic, mechanical, photocopying, recording or otherwise, without the prior permission of the publisher.

British Library Cataloguing in Publication Data
A catalogue record for this book is available from the British Library.

ISBN 978-1-915046-95-6

Unless otherwise indicated, Scripture quotations taken from New International Version, (Anglicised edition).
Copyright ©1979, 1984, 2011 by Biblica.
Used by permission of Hodder & Stoughton Publishers, an Hachette UK company. All rights reserved.
'NIV' is a registered trademark of Biblica.
UK trademark number 1448790.

Scripture quotations marked MSG are taken from *THE MESSAGE*, copyright © 1993, 2002, 2018 by Eugene H. Peterson.
Used by permission of NavPress. All rights reserved.
Represented by Tyndale House Publishers, Inc.

Scripture quotations marked NLT are taken from the *Holy Bible*, New Living Translation, copyright © 1996, 2004, 2015 by Tyndale House Foundation. Used by permission of Tyndale House Publishers, Inc., Carol Stream, Illinois 60188. All rights reserved.

Quotations and extract from *Restoration Magazine* in Chapters Three and Four used with permission
'Be Still' by Dave Evans in Chapter Seven, © 1986 Kingsway's Thankyou Music
Quotation from *Arthur Wallis: Radical Christian* by Jonathan Wallis in Chapter Nine used with permission

Quotation from *Red Moon Rising* by Pete Greig in Chapter Thirteen used with permission

While every effort has been made to contact those named in this book, it has not always been possible to locate people.

Cover design by David Kennedy Form Productions
www.form.london

Printed in the UK

Dedication

To the *REMAINERS* – the men and women who have been part of this church community for many years, some from day one, who still meet every Monday morning to pray for the church, its mission and its leadership. This is your story.

Commendations

It's inspirational to read an adventure story like this about a community pioneering, again and again, over half a century to impact Southampton, the nation and the nations. My life has been changed by this church because it was here in Southampton at the Cultural Shift conference that the 24-7 Prayer movement was born. We are forever grateful.

Pete Greig, founder, 24-7 Prayer International, senior pastor, Emmaus Road Church

This book tracks the timeline of New Community Church, Southampton, providing a written testimony to God's faithfulness over the last five decades. The first few chapters provide fascinating insights into the history of the early charismatic movement and describe the remarkable ways that God worked, by renewing and shaping his Church. It was into this context that New Community Church was birthed. The rest of the book records the opportunities and challenges, the key people playing their part and how the early dreams and vision of the founding members were gradually outworked year by year and decade by decade. The collective kingdom impact of New Community Church over fifty years is significant, touching and transforming individuals, families, estates, schools and many spheres of influence within the city and beyond.

Ness Wilson, Pioneer UK leader

This is a book which does not sugarcoat church life. It tells an honest and, at times, painful story of the delights, joys and encouragements of a community of faith, alongside the struggles, disappointments and, even, failures. Through it all I'm left thankful to God for New Community Church, Southampton. This is a story of faith and resilience with a deep conviction that they had been called by him to express his life into their city and beyond.

Steve Clifford, former general director of the Evangelical Alliance, chair of the Pioneer Board

What a gift this book is. To those who lived this story, to those who observed, and for those who enjoy the fruit of the lives written about in this book, this is a stone of remembrance and a foundation stone.

This is a story which needs telling, because the testimony of Jesus must not be lost in the sea of information and experience which our modern digital world has given us. It must not be lost in the assumption that because we know names and places we know the narrative or remotely understand the price which was paid for what we can enjoy today.

It is so easy to assume that we know a story because of the highlights, but this book gives us the shadows too, the places and times which involved a battle, a price and a step of faith. The stories of discovering the Holy Spirit, the prophetic, the developing experience of his presence are a rich backdrop and antidote to taking our own experiences for granted.

We need this story, not for nostalgia, but for where we as a Church and nation need to go. We need this story to become a prophecy for tomorrow.

Paul Manwaring, senior leadership team, Bethel Church, Redding, California

New Community Church stands out as an example of obedience and resilience in the Church today. It's amazing to see the lives God has changed around the corner and across the world – through the faithfulness of this one obedient church. May their story encourage you further in fearless obedience.

Alan Scott, senior pastor, The Dwelling Place, Anaheim, California, USA

Billy Kennedy is an ecumenical giant. As a former president of Churches Together in England, his influence over the wider Church cannot be understated. This is a powerful story that will inspire the reader to understand that God can work through his church again and again and again. A must-read!

Bishop Mike Royal, general secretary, Churches Together in England

Our time at New Community Church from our arrival as students in the late seventies to our departure to help plant a new church in East Sussex in the early nineties revolutionised our Christian lives. The presence of God, the call to radical discipleship and community and the powerful prophetic preaching gave us a vision of the beauty of the local church that took our breath away.

Janet and I met in my first ever church midweek group meeting and now, forty-five years later we have the privilege of leading King's Community Church in Southampton, one of the many churches that were birthed out of what the Holy Spirit did during a remarkable move of God fifty years ago. We are so grateful to God for our time as part of New Community.

Andy Johnston, senior pastor, King's Community Church

I love honesty, and this book provides exactly that. It's the story of a Christ-centred community and their fifty-year journey of vision and faithfulness, frustration, setback, tragedy yet hope. And through it all there has been breakthrough and progress, of which Oasis has had an opportunity to be just a little part.

Now the story of the next fifty years begins!

Rev. Steve Chalke MBE, founder of Oasis Trust

I am so pleased that this church story is being told. I have fond memories of visits and exchange of ministries. My path crossed with many mentioned in the book. Tony Stone shared a word that helped direct me into ministry. Jean Darnall became like a spiritual mother to me, and I enjoyed friendship with Tony Morton.

This book openly and honestly charts the journey of a highly influential church that has navigated its seasons wisely. It is good to see a new generation of leaders continue to guide the church into its jubilee season and this reflects the multi-coloured grace of God.

Stuart Bell, senior pastor, Alive Church, founder, Ground Level Network

What a stirring book about a fifty-year-old innovative church community, strongly characterised by Word and Spirit, loving its native city of Southampton well, and proving a huge inspiration to me and many others. My friend Billy's volume insightfully highlights the peaks and troughs of life for the fellowship, likening it to a tapestry of blessing woven by heaven, and one reflecting God's kindly rule on earth. In particular, I was provoked to think more deeply about what revival really looks like, and to yearn for a Church today that better worships Jesus, forms disciples, rescues wanderers and transforms society. Thoroughly un-put-downable!

Andrew Whitman, lifelong pastor, revival historian, and author of When Jesus Met Hippies

I owe so much to my time at Southampton Community Church! Not only did I meet my amazing wife, Sarah, there, but I also got to be part of a group of people making a real difference in the lives of the people and communities in the city.

As a young student trying to find my place in the world, battling with low self-esteem and low self-confidence, the church was an amazing body of people giving incredible teaching and insights and a closeness to God that has shaped and formed who I am today. So many of my core beliefs, principles and values were shaped over my six years in the church in the early to mid-1990s and for that I am forever grateful.

It's fair to say that my life is more fulfilled, richer and better for my time at Southampton Community Church, and I feel blessed and thankful that I got to be part of such an exciting movement at such an exciting time – here's to the next fifty years!

Pete Markey, chief marketing officer, Walgreens Boots Alliance

In April 1996, I watched *Songs of Praise* from Central Hall, Southampton. The next morning, I could still hear the people singing 'My Jesus, My Saviour' and I burst into tears. I cried out, 'I want to serve a church like that!' That prayer was a turning point. Six months later, I was appointed leader of St Andrew's, Chorleywood, a church just like the one I'd seen in Southampton.

It's therefore such a joy to read and commend Billy's account of a church to which I owe a lasting debt – a church and movement which I had the privilege of ministering to several times in the years that followed. This book tells the honest and inspiring story of a wonderful move of God – one which will cause those involved to be grateful for the past and hopeful for the future.

Dr Mark Stibbe, award-winning author

Frank and I were senior pastors at Ivy Church, Manchester and we craved a network to belong to. In the early 2000s we found c.net. It was like home for us. Frank's passion for theology was recognised and my yearning to be part of a prophetic network was fulfilled. We started attending the leaders' conferences at Central Hall and they breathed life into our calling.

I always remember someone saying 'Ivy is a resource church', which was a perfect description of what we were, but we hadn't realised. The first conference felt like an oasis in a desert for us, and I cried most of the way through it. We belonged, made friends for life and we are forever grateful.

Debra Green OBE, DL, founder and executive director, Redeeming Our Communities

We need more stories like this! Stories of his Church where Jesus stays at the centre. Where we trust him to build his Church and each generation experiences the presence and the person of Jesus, as opposed to programmes and formulae. Well done, and we are excited to be a part of what he is still building today through New Community Church.

Chris Abington, senior leader, City Church, Russellville, Arkansas, USA

Generations Generations Generations tells the fascinating story of a small group of people who decided to allow their lives to be shaped by God's Word and the leading of the Holy

Spirit. The adventure that unfolded led to many changed lives, a city that would never be quite the same and people who could no longer settle for anything less than God's best.

I've known Billy Kennedy for most of this time. His integrity and love for God have always shone through. He's refused to ever settle for an easy life. You will be inspired and provoked, as you read this book, to live in the same way.

David Stroud, co-founder, the Everything Network and founding pastor, Christ Church London

Over the years, New Community Church, Southampton has left a deep and lasting impression on my life. It's remarkable to see how God has moved through the faith and obedience of a people who entrusted their lives to him, shaping a community that listens to the Spirit and responds boldly to the needs of the world. This story is a testament to hope, resilience and God's faithfulness. Billy captures the journey with clarity and heart, offering a narrative that inspires anyone longing to build a Spirit-led, mission-focused community. It's a journey with many rich chapters, and undoubtedly, more to come.

Brian Heasley, international director of prayer, 24-7 Prayer

Alison and I met Billy and Caroline Kennedy in our early days in Southampton. A great friendship quickly formed which lasted through nearly two decades as church leaders in the city. Whatever our differences in background and (occasionally) understanding, I always saw in Billy and Caroline a deep, infectious love for Jesus and his Church and a bold commitment to local mission, both of which I admired greatly. It has been a great joy to work with them. This arresting book tells the story of the remarkable ways God has worked through the church they served and led.

John Risbridger, director, Catalyst Leadership and Theology Course, formerly minister and team leader of Above Bar Church Southampton

Generations Generations Generations is a beautiful story of God's kindness and mercy for his people. It continues to be written in and through the gracious members and ministries of Community Church, a congregation that warmly welcomed this stranger many years ago. Their kindness and devotion to Jesus shine as a signal fire of grace, and the leadership of Billy Kennedy has been instrumental in that light burning brightly for so long. I believe it will inspire you as it has inspired me.

David Cassidy, Lead Pastor, Spanish River Church, Boca Raton, Florida

Contents

Acknowledgements   19
Introduction   21

Chapter One: The Day It All Began   27

Chapter Two: Beginnings   33

Chapter Three: Part of Something Bigger   49

Chapter Four: Tony Morton   65

Chapter Five: Finding My Feet   79

Chapter Six: Words, Works and Wonders   91

Chapter Seven: Gains and Losses   103

Chapter Eight: What About the Women?   117

Chapter Nine: Growth and Influence   129

Chapter Ten: Big Church   139

Chapter Eleven: Adjusting to the New   149

Chapter Twelve: Toronto   161

Chapter Thirteen: Cutting Edge   175

Chapter Fourteen: A Weaving of Ministries   195

Chapter Fifteen: A New Shape Emerges   207

Chapter Sixteen: All Together Now   217

Chapter Seventeen: Transition	229
Chapter Eighteen: The First Year	239
Chapter Nineteen: Double Whammy!	251
Chapter Twenty: Wisdom and Words	263
Chapter Twenty-one: A New Season	275
Chapter Twenty-two: Education, Education, Education	287
Chapter Twenty-three: New Partners	299
Chapter Twenty-four: Love and Buses	311
Chapter Twenty-five: Hope for the City	323
Chapter Twenty-six: Seasons of Fruitfulness	337
Chapter Twenty-seven: Fifty Years and Counting	351
For Further Reading	363
Further Information	366
Endnotes	367

Acknowledgements

As always with a project such as this, there are many people to thank. I'd like to start by thanking all those who helped me in my research of the church's early years for the book: Roy Pearson, Mike and Jane Evans, Hannah Strutt, Phil and Sheelagh Clarke, Martyn Dunsford and Kathy Swift all provided invaluable insights. I'd like to acknowledge John Fleming's retelling of the story of the formation of the church in his book, *Bind us Together*, and Brian Hewitt's extensive interview with Tony Morton in his 1995 publication, *Doing a New Thing*, helped enormously in the writing of Chapter Four.

My co-author, Ralph Turner, has been a constant source of support, encouragement and, at times, challenge. I wouldn't have completed the project without him. I'd like to thank Alison Leigh and Nathan Turner for their work in proofreading, and my dear friend of more than forty years, Phil Orchard, who read the draft manuscript to fact check the story but inevitably helped with crossing 't's, dotting 'i's and making sure the apostrophes were in the right place!

A big thanks, too, to all who supported the Kickstarter campaign to get the book published. In particular, Ben and

Jo Popplestone, Jonathan and Katrina Cathie and Stuart and Lou Thom deserve special mention for their generosity.

And finally, to the numerous leaders and volunteers who have faithfully served alongside for so many years, thank you. We wouldn't have made it without you.

Introduction

This book is a story told from my perspective – a personal and reflective account of the journey of New Community Church, Southampton, and the broader community and networks it has been involved in. Having been part of this church since 1982, a member of its ministry leadership team since 1984, and senior leader from 2002 until 2022, I've had the privilege of witnessing firsthand the remarkable evolution of this community. While many voices could tell their own versions of this story, what follows is my unique and subjective view, shaped by four decades of involvement. This is not just a history of events, but a personal reflection on the joys, struggles and transformations that have made this church what it is today.

When I joined what was then called Southampton Community Church in 1982, it was already a vibrant, growing church shaped by the energy of charismatic renewal and the emerging house church movement. I could not have known at that time how integral this community would become in my life, or the crucial role I would eventually play in its leadership. But from the very beginning, I was captivated by the church's commitment to the pursuit of the presence of God and the deep sense of authentic Christian community. These were people passionate about following Jesus and I was drawn to the quality of relationships and the boldness of their vision.

As I stepped into my first leadership role in 1984, I quickly learned that leading a church is not without its challenges. Growth brings both opportunities and difficulties, and the journey from those early days to the community we know today has been filled with moments of celebration as well as times of hardship. One thing I have committed to in writing this account is not to sweep the difficult moments under the carpet. I believe that the true story of New Community Church includes the highs and the lows, the victories and the valleys, because each has shaped who we are as a church.

One of the most difficult periods we faced was the sudden departure of our former senior leader in 2004. This was a moment of significant transition and pain for the church, as any leadership change of that magnitude inevitably brings. The departure was not without its challenges – questions of direction, identity and leadership stability weighed heavily on our community. During that time, I had to navigate the church through uncertainty and the process was both humbling and refining for all of us. I won't pretend it was easy, but in the end, it was a turning point that allowed us to refocus on the heart of our mission and prepare for the future.

This commitment to transparency is central to how I've sought to lead the church and it is how I've approached telling this story. I don't believe in painting an idealised picture of the past. The history of New Community Church is a real one – marked by seasons of great joy and growth, but also by moments of struggle, disappointment and even failure. Yet through it all, God's faithfulness has remained a constant and it is that faithfulness that continues to sustain us.

In the early years, the church's rapid growth was exhilarating. By the late 1970s and early 1980s, what began as Southampton Christian Fellowship had grown far beyond its humble beginnings, attracting people from all over the city and region, with ministry opportunities opening up in many nations. As new leaders emerged, the church became increasingly influential, both locally and as part of the broader Restoration movement – a network of churches dedicated to restoring New Testament practices of worship, community and spiritual gifts. This was initially, through the development of the Cornerstone, or c.net, network, and later on, in our role at the heart of the Pioneer network. This period of dynamic growth saw us move into our current home at Central Hall in the heart of the city and develop new ministries. But as with any growing organisation, challenges arose as we sought to manage this expansion while staying true to our core values.

By the time I stepped into the role of senior leader in 2002, the church was poised for another season of change. The name change to New Community Church in 2007 was more than a rebranding exercise; it reflected our renewed vision to be a church that actively served our city, built relationships and continued to pursue the Holy Spirit's leading. We wanted to make it clear that we were a church committed to our local community, with a heart for social justice and a desire to be a welcoming and inclusive family for all who came through our doors.

The decision to change the name marked the beginning of a new chapter, but it also reminded us that our core values – prioritising God's presence, authentic community and the transformative power of the gospel – remained unchanged. While we embraced a broader mission, the foundations that had been laid by the earlier generations continued to guide us.

Looking back, I can see how every challenge and transition has been part of a larger narrative of growth and maturity. The moments of difficulty – whether they were leadership transitions, cultural shifts or internal struggles – have taught us resilience and deepened our faith. These moments have also reminded us of the importance of community. One of the greatest strengths of New Community Church has always been its people – the men, women and families who have committed to living out their faith together in genuine relationships.

This book is not only a reflection on the church's history but also a testament to those individuals who, through their faith, sacrifices and perseverance, have helped build this community. It's their stories that bring this history to life. I've watched as friendships have deepened, families have been formed and lives have been transformed. I've also witnessed how the church has continued to play an essential role in the wider city of Southampton, engaging with issues of poverty, social justice and community transformation. And we've continued to be active in playing our part as members of a wider international apostolic movement.

Introduction

As I reflect on my time leading this church, I do so with a profound sense of gratitude. These last forty years have been a journey of faith, filled with unexpected twists, moments of uncertainty and times of celebration. My hope in writing this book is that it not only captures the journey we've been on as a church but also serves as an encouragement to future generations. The story of New Community Church is far from over. God is still at work, and the seeds planted in the 1970s continue to bear fruit today, from one generation to the next.

I invite you to read these pages not just as a historical record, but as a living testament to what God has done – and continues to do – through his people. This is a story of faith, resilience and the unshakable belief that God can use ordinary people to accomplish extraordinary things. Whether you've been part of the church for decades, or are just discovering our story, my prayer is that you will be inspired by what has been and excited for what is yet to come.

Billy Kennedy
February 2025
Southampton

Chapter One

THE DAY IT ALL BEGAN

It's Sunday, 2nd March 1975.

Steve Harley and Cockney Rebel are at number one in the charts with *Make Me Smile (Come Up and See Me)*. Donald Coggan has recently been enthroned as the Archbishop of Canterbury.

Just two days before, on Friday, 28th February, a major London tube train crash at Moorgate station had killed forty-three people and injured a further seventy-four. The tragedy had cast a shadow over the city, with newspapers filled with stories of the victims and heroic rescues.

Harold Wilson was the prime minister. Just a few weeks before, Margaret Thatcher had defeated Edward Heath for the leadership of the Conservative Party, becoming the party's first female leader. This political shift was stirring conversations across the nation, with many speculating on how Thatcher's leadership might change the course of British politics.

In the world of sport, Dave Mackay's Derby County were on course to win their second Division One league title. In rugby union, Scotland had beaten Wales the previous day, 12-10 at Murrayfield, watched by a world record attendance of 104,000 in the Five Nations Championship. And Muhammad Ali had recently defeated Chuck Wepner in a boxing match on 24th February, a fight that would later inspire the movie *Rocky*.

And in cinemas, audiences were flocking to see *The Towering Inferno*, a disaster film that had captured the public's imagination.

Ragtag group

It was also the day that a ragtag group of Jesus followers, adopting the name Southampton Christian Fellowship, would meet for the first time. The idea of forming a new church had been bubbling under the surface for some time, and today was the day it would come to fruition.

Roy Pearson, one of the organisers, worked for Hampshire County Council and was tasked with finding a suitable venue for the meeting. Ideally, the group would prefer a school hall, but Roy couldn't find any caretaker willing to work on a Sunday. After much searching and numerous phone calls, he had to settle with the Social Centre for the Blind on The Avenue, close to the university. The centre was not perfect, but it was available and would serve their needs for now.

The meeting was planned to start at 3.00 p.m. Roy and his wife, Gillian, along with their three children, Mike, Julie and Jamie, arrived just before 2.00 p.m. to collect the key. They opened the building and arranged the chairs in a horseshoe shape, leaving lots of space in the centre. The cold, institutional smell of the centre was quickly replaced by the warmth of excited conversation as more people began to arrive.

Rodney pitched up with his guitar, together with his wife, Edna. 'Do you think anyone will actually come?' Edna asked, her voice tinged with nervous excitement.

'We'll see,' Rodney replied, tuning his guitar, 'but I have a good feeling about this.'

Ron and Evelyn turned up with the refreshments. Evelyn had made some cheese and onion sandwiches, carefully wrapped in wax paper. Carolyn couldn't make it, but she sent some cakes, freshly baked that morning. John, Jean and Julian were there, each bringing their own sense of anticipation. Tony had travelled down from Teddington in his Triumph Toledo, determined not to miss this inaugural meeting.

Conversations began about how many people they thought might attend. Twenty? Thirty? Maybe forty? The uncertainty added to the sense of adventure.

Questions

Slowly people began to arrive, many curious about this new venture. They came with their questions.

'Is it OK to start a new church? How is it going to work? Is there a minister?' whispered a young student to his friend.

Some just came to see what was going on, drawn by the buzz of something new happening.

It was 3.00 p.m.

Time to start.

Around fifty people were now crammed into the room. A couple of students had also brought their guitars. Andy unpacked his recorder. And there were lots of tambourines. The room was filled with a vibrant mix of denim, flares, platform shoes, long hair, beards, Laura Ashley dresses and headscarves!

Ron Rothery, only one of two men wearing a tie, welcomed everyone and invited people to stand to begin to worship. On the striking of the first chord, the worship began. There was no need to warm people up. The room was immediately filled with the sound of the combined voices and the few instruments. There was lots of joy, and most were dancing. It was heavenly.

Spontaneous

People began contributing spontaneously with prayers, prophecy and words of encouragement. There was no recognised worship leader as such, no 'set list', no platform to focus on, just voices, a recorder and a few guitars in harmony, flowing together.

Ian McCulloch, the leader of a small house church in the town of Emsworth thirty miles along the coast, and the one who had been charged with overseeing the new group, stood up, opened his Bible, and shared on the 'love of God'. His words resonated with those gathered, many nodding in agreement or closing their eyes in contemplation.

It was 5.00 p.m.

Time for tea. Those with children left to put them to bed. Everyone else remained, not wanting to miss a moment of this new experience.

6.00 p.m. Time to start again.

Roy led this session. Once again, the worship 'took off'. The presence of God filled the room. Everyone was caught up with a sense of awe. There were more contributions from those gathered.

Ian got up again and shared from the Scriptures on 'renewing the mind'. His talk finished. Silence. Nobody moved. The weight of his words hung in the air, giving everyone pause for reflection.

Someone began a song. Everyone joined in. People were now on their feet singing in the Spirit. No set words. Simply voices in unison, harmonising, rising to a crescendo, becoming quiet, rising again. Songs of the heart.

It's 8.30 p.m. No one wants to leave. Roy closed the meeting, reminding people that the church would meet again next Sunday, same time, same place. He encouraged everyone to bring a friend. People nodded enthusiastically, already looking forward to the next gathering.

It was time to go.

As people made their way out, the conversation was around what had just happened. 'What an incredible start,' Roy said to Gillian as they gathered their things. 'I couldn't have imagined it going any better. I think it could be the start of something special.'

Just how special it would become would unfold over the next fifty years, but tonight the journey had just begun. A remarkable journey. With many highs and lows, joys and sorrows, laughter and tears. But a journey that no one in the room on that Sunday afternoon could ever have imagined.

Chapter Two

BEGINNINGS

Although 2nd March was the first official meeting of the Southampton Christian Fellowship, the story begins much earlier.

Once upon a time ...

There were a number of strands that had led to this moment. The first was what became known as the charismatic movement, and another, the desire for an authentic and vibrant expression of church life that was being explored by influential characters in what became the house church or Restoration movement.

The charismatic renewal was a global movement that brought the experience of the baptism in the Holy Spirit beyond the traditional Pentecostal churches, invigorating many mainstream denominations. This renewal movement was marked by a fresh encounter with God, a freedom in worship expression, a renewed confidence in the gospel, an outpouring of spiritual gifts and a deeper sense of community.

The charismatic movement was not orchestrated by any single individual or organisation. It had many key figures and moments that catalysed its spread, especially in the decades following the Second World War – a time of post-war recovery where people were searching for meaning, deeper spiritual experiences and a greater sense of community. This era was characterised by a longing for spiritual revival and authenticity, a backdrop against which the charismatic renewal found fertile ground.

Key people

During the 1940s and 1950s, several notable individuals played crucial roles in the growth of the charismatic renewal and the house church movement across the United Kingdom.

Cecil Cousens, based in Bradford, was a former Apostolic Church minister influenced by the Latter Rain Movement in Canada. His ministry was marked by a deep hunger for spiritual revival and a passion for the gifts of the Holy Spirit.

David Lillie, a member of the Plymouth Brethren in Exeter, received the fullness of the Spirit in 1941. His experience signalled a departure from the traditionally cessationist views of the Plymouth Brethren, embracing a more dynamic and experiential faith.

Sidney Purse, baptised in the Holy Spirit in the late 1940s, began a house church in his home in South Chard, Somerset. His gatherings became a hub for those seeking deeper spiritual experiences.

Pastor Wally North established Calvary Holiness Church in Bradford in 1952. The network of churches he formed were influential in the development of the charismatic renewal and house church movements across the nation.

Campbell McAlpine and Denis Clark, South African ministers, moved to England in the mid-1950s and ministered extensively, helping many receive the baptism in the Holy Spirit.

These individuals, and others, shared a common experience of the Holy Spirit but did not align with traditional Pentecostal denominations, marking the beginnings of a fresh spiritual awakening mirrored globally. Their ministries laid the groundwork for a broader acceptance of charismatic practices within various Christian traditions.

Global influences

In 1936, David du Plessis was appointed general secretary of the South African-based Apostolic Faith Mission at the age of thirty-one. Initially describing himself as a 'sectarian' Pentecostal, du Plessis' outlook changed dramatically after meeting Smith Wigglesworth, a British evangelist known for his powerful healing ministry. Wigglesworth prophesied a revival that would transcend previous movements, filling churches and fields with worshippers.

Du Plessis worked with Donald Gee, a key leader in the Assemblies of God in Great Britain and Ireland, promoting cooperation among Pentecostal groups and organising the first Pentecostal World Conference in 1947. Moving away from his Pentecostal sectarian roots, du Plessis advocated ecumenism, sharing the Pentecostal experience with historic Christian denominations, particularly Roman Catholics. His work significantly linked traditional Pentecostal churches with the emerging neo-Pentecostal charismatic movement.

Arthur Wallis

Arthur Wallis was a key voice and influence in both the charismatic renewal and house church movement and was especially influential for the newly formed church in Southampton.

Son of evangelist Captain Reginald Wallis, Arthur attended Monkton Combe School, the Royal Military Academy at Sandhurst, and served in the Royal Tank Regiment during wartime. Following his military service, Wallis pursued itinerant preaching in south-west England.

In 1951, inspired by Dr R.A. Torrey's article on the baptism in the Holy Spirit,[1] Wallis experienced a profound encounter with the Holy Spirit in his study. He did not speak in tongues straight away but knew he had been filled with the Spirit. Wallis, along with his friend and colleague, David Lillie, organised a small conference in 1952 to explore the nature of the church. This gathering of about twenty-five leaders was transformative, emphasising the need for revival and appropriate vessels to contain it – a church uncompromised and committed to fulfilling God's purposes.

In 1958, Wallis and Lillie hosted another significant conference in Devon, The Church of Jesus Christ – Its Purity, Power, Pattern, and Programme in the Context of Today. This event featured several guest speakers including Roger Forster, who would later form Ichthus Christian Fellowship. A subsequent conference in 1961 focused on The Divine Purpose in the Institution of the Church, where Wallis expressed his vision for a church free from denominational structures.

Charismatic renewal in the USA and the UK

In the USA, Dennis Bennett's announcement in 1960 that he had been filled with the Holy Spirit and spoken in tongues brought widespread attention to the charismatic movement. Bennett's resignation from St Mark's Episcopal Church in California and the surrounding controversy sparked interest in the movement across the water in the United Kingdom.

Michael Harper, a young curate at All Souls, Langham Place, London, experienced the baptism in the Holy Spirit in 1962, leading to conflicts with his vicar, John Stott. Harper left All Souls in 1964 and founded the Fountain Trust, which was hugely instrumental in promoting personal and church renewal across the United Kingdom.

Also in 1962, Bryn Jones attended one of the conferences hosted by Wallis and Lillie, where news of the breakthroughs in the Episcopalian Church in the USA was discussed. Jones, a fiery Welshman, became a good friend and colleague of Arthur Wallis, and a prominent leader in the house church movement of the late 1960s and early 1970s.

In 1965, Wallis, Lillie and Campbell McAlpine organised a conference at Herne Bay Court, Kent, titled The Apostolic Commission – The Message, the Men, and the Methods. This significant gathering brought together future key leaders in the new church movement, including Terry Virgo, Barney Coombs, John Noble and Peter Lyne.

By the late 1960s, the charismatic renewal was spreading to the Roman Catholic Church, notably through the 1967 Duquesne Weekend in Pittsburgh, USA, which ignited the Catholic Charismatic Renewal. Similar movements emerged at universities across the USA, including Michigan State and Notre Dame, creating a global influence. This spread indicated a profound shift in the religious landscape, as the charismatic renewal transcended denominational boundaries and brought a fresh dynamism to Christian worship.

The Jesus Movement

Alongside this activity within the mainstream denominations and among those who were seeking a more authentic expression of church was what has been described as 'The Jesus Movement'. This movement started among the youth counterculture in North America around 1967 but soon spread to many other nations. The terms 'Jesus Movement' or 'Jesus People' were used to describe these young people turning to Christ and transforming their lifestyles, a movement so influential it made the cover of *Time Magazine* in June 1971.

The Jesus Movement was characterised by its informal and grassroots nature. It was a movement driven by young people disillusioned with traditional religious structures and seeking a more personal and direct experience of God. The Jesus Movement contributed to the broader charismatic renewal by emphasising a vibrant, community-focused Christianity that resonated with a generation seeking authenticity and change.

Southampton Christian Fellowship

All these influences formed the backdrop to the formation of this new Southampton church – the charismatic experience, the desire for a more authentic expression of church and the hunger among many young people for deeper spirituality and community.

And so it was, on 2nd March 1975, three groups in Southampton – Pentecostals, who were looking for a more authentic expression of church; Baptists, who had received a dramatic baptism in the Holy Spirit; and university students, swept along with fresh zeal and enthusiasm – joined to form the Southampton Christian Fellowship.

The Agape Fellowship

Martyn Dunsford came to Southampton university in September 1970. He was from an unchurched background but by the end of his first year he had become a Christian. He returned for his second year and began to attend the university Christian Union. He was appointed as president of the Christian Union in 1972. The membership of the Christian Union was very conservative and at that time strongly opposed the charismatic renewal. This began to create some tensions when Martyn was baptised in the Holy Spirit during his term as president.

To provide a place for those who wanted a more open expression of worship, he and several other fellow students started to gather on a Saturday afternoon for worship before the main Christian Union meeting in the evening. This informal group became known as the Agape Fellowship and, before long, was attracting more than seventy students.

Martyn and other students found a welcoming environment at Kendal Avenue Pentecostal Church, led by Tony and Sheila Stone. Dunsford developed a close friendship with an elder, Ron Rothery, who also led the Full Gospel Businessmen's Fellowship in Southampton. Ron had met Bryn Jones at a conference in 1973 and invited him to Southampton. Martyn met Bryn for the first time during this visit and invited him to come and speak at the Agape Fellowship.

These meetings were key to what was to follow. Bryn, influenced by Arthur Wallis and others in those early meetings, was developing what for many in the church at the time was a new concept – that of the apostle. Arthur had developed this idea and Bryn took it further. Bryn believed that the role of the apostle and the prophet had not died out with the early Church as had been commonly taught, but that these gifts were essential to the future expansion of the church.

With this in mind, Bryn began to develop his own apostolic ministry, based initially in the Bradford area, where he was based, but extending further as his team grew.

In the summer of 1974, Martyn's university course finished and he was invited by Bryn to move to Bradford to be part of the growing church and ministry there. By this time, Tony Morton had emerged as a key leader within the Agape Fellowship. Tony's university course had also finished, and he had taken a job in London but was travelling back to Southampton every weekend. He, together with Julian Boden and others, took responsibility for the group of students meeting on campus.

Bitterne Park

In the early 1970s, several people from a local Baptist church in Bitterne Park experienced the baptism in the Holy Spirit and began meeting at Roy and Gillian Pearson's home. These gatherings attracted many seeking the Holy Spirit, eventually leading to their departure from the Baptist church and integration with Kendal Avenue Pentecostal Church.

When Bryn Jones visited Southampton in 1973, he stayed with Roy and Gillian and prophesied over them:

> I have seen the hunger in your hearts, the longing for more of my kingdom. I will build my church here and I will add to you many who are hungry for my presence, many more who you do not yet know and many others who are not yet part of my kingdom.

The seeds for what was about to happen were being sown.

Changes at Kendal Avenue

Around this time, Tony and Sheila Stone, the pastors of Kendal Avenue Pentecostal Church, had responded to a call to go into full-time evangelism with British Youth for Christ. Therefore, they announced that they would be leaving the church.

Tony and Sheila had been hosting meetings in their home on Sunday evenings for those seeking to grow in spiritual gifts and the charismatic experience. This informal gathering attracted quite a few of the students and former students who were or had been part of the Agape Fellowship.

Ron Rothery and his wife, Evelyn, felt it would be good to continue these meetings after Tony and Sheila moved away, so they opened their home to the group.

But by late 1974 it became clear that the elders at Kendal Avenue Pentecostal Church were unhappy with the meetings in Ron and Evelyn's home and did not agree with the new ideas on the nature of church that Ron and the group were embracing. With a heavy heart and after much soul-searching, Ron decided to step down as an elder at the church.

The meeting with Bryn

Ron and Evelyn, along with Roy and Gillian, organised a meeting with Bryn Jones and Dave Mansell, who was part of Bryn's apostolic team, on 9th February 1975, at the home of Rodney and Edna Martin, one of the young couples who were part of the Baptist church in Bitterne Park. As well as Ron, Roy and Rodney, the two main leaders of the Agape student group attended the meeting: Tony Morton, who would go on to serve as the senior leader of the church for the next twenty-five years, and Julian Boden, a fellow student. Also attending was a former student, now attending the Kendal Avenue Pentecostal Church, John Fleming.

Each described to Bryn what was happening – the growing blessing of the Holy Spirit on their meetings, the tensions with other churches around the issue of baptism in the Spirit and the sense they had about the beginning of something new.

Bryn listened. Leaning forward with a smile on his face, he commented, 'Well, I wonder what God is doing here. Clearly, he's bringing you together and there is more to come. Can I encourage you to keep going with your midweek ministries and meetings – Ron and John in the west of the city, Roy and Rodney in the east, Tony and Julian with the students.

'But then, I think you should also start meeting together on Sundays and form a new church. Look for a venue and plan to meet. The time is right.'

Bryn proposed Ron as the leader of the new venture, supported by Ian McCulloch, who was leading a small house church along the coast in Emsworth. Many of the students already knew Ian, who was now a member of Bryn's wider apostolic team.

Rapid growth

Week two at the Social Centre for the Blind saw the arrival of more students. And as the weeks passed, there were more still, as well as increasing numbers of couples and families from other churches.

The format remained the same. Open worship, shared words as people felt God was speaking to them, testimonies, followed by a prepared word from one of the new leaders. Fellowship over shared meals meant the beginning of shared lives and new friendships, all linked still to the growing midweek home meetings.

The new church rapidly outgrew the Social Centre for the Blind and by the end of May, after only a few short weeks, the church meeting had moved to The Gregg School in Winn Road.

Most of the congregation were under thirty, with a high percentage of students now attending regularly. In the first year, some tensions began to emerge between Bryn and Ian, and there were also some discussions around the leadership styles of Ian and Ron, who were quite a bit older than the rest of the group and of a different generation.

In early 1976 Bryn came to visit again and met with the 'unofficial' leadership group at Tony's flat. He announced that Ian would no longer be providing covering for the church, but that Bryn would do that himself and that he had also invited Ron and Evelyn to move to Bradford to be involved in a refurbishment project of Church House, the Bradford church's new facility.

The final piece of the jigsaw was that the informal leadership team would be disbanded, and Tony Morton would now become the main leader of the church.

Southampton Community Church

Tony had recently married Hannah, and both had enrolled at the La Sainte Union teacher training college in Southampton. After a year they both got jobs in local schools. Tony was juggling responsibilities as a new husband, newly qualified teacher and leader of a fast-growing church. And he was only in his mid-twenties!

There was such momentum in these first few years as people began to experience authentic Christian community and a genuine spirituality. It was attractive, and more and more people were becoming a part of it.

Another church in the city, West End Evangelical Church, had been birthed several years before as a result of an evangelistic mission. The new church was gifted some land by a local Christian farmer to build a church building. They too had experienced the baptism in the Holy Spirit and had developed a connection with Arthur Wallis.

It was Arthur who suggested they merge with the newly formed Southampton Christian Fellowship, and after much prayer and discussion the merger took place in 1977, and the new church changed its name to Southampton Community Church.

Bob Hall, the leader of the West End Evangelical Church, joined Tony as co-leader of the newly formed Southampton Community Church. However, that leadership partnership did not last long, and it was at this point that Bryn appointed the first official elders in the church to work alongside Tony: Geoff Wright and Roger Popplestone, both secondary school teachers, Peter Light, who took on the role of church administrator and Mick Caws, a local business owner.

The church moved its Sunday meeting to the Bitterne Park secondary school and by the late 1970s, more than 250 people were gathering each Sunday. People were now travelling to be part of the church from across the region – from Totton, Romsey, Winchester, Eastleigh, Gosport, Hedge End, and even further afield.

What was so attractive?

There were probably three things that were attracting people to this fledgling church.

Firstly, there was an insatiable hunger for the presence of God. The baptism in the Holy Spirit and the use of spiritual gifts contextualised in this new cultural moment brought a freshness and a freedom to the worship experience.

This was a radical departure from normal church life. Most churches operated some form of traditional liturgy. This was either in the form of the traditional Anglo-Catholic prayer book or the non-conformist 'hymn-prayer-sandwich' evident in most Baptist, Methodist or other independent churches.

This was fresh. It was a new sound that was reflecting and providing a narrative for what God was doing. Worship could normally last for an hour or even longer wherever people gathered. The experience of many was that worship in the home or student flat was as dynamic an experience as when they gathered in the larger setting.

Secondly, there was a strong emphasis to live out a genuine, everyday Christian faith in close-knit communities. Acts 2:42-47 and Acts 4:32-37 became key passages for the fledgling community. Scriptures that were being outworked in their daily lives. The 'believers' were there for each other, supporting one another, meeting together almost daily, sharing life over meals, helping anyone in need. These weren't just words on a page, this was their lived experience.

Many of the students had been living in shared houses and so deep friendships were formed that continued as the students went into work, got married and had children.

There was a desire to see the body of Christ operating day to day, week by week and to see church not just limited to a Sunday worship gathering, but out in their neighbourhoods, in and around the city.

And thirdly, there was a vision for what church could be. A place where disciples were formed, free from legalistic practices and limiting structures; where people were encouraged and equipped to make a difference in their neighbourhoods and communities. And there was a growing hope and expectation that this would result in many conversions and societal transformation.

The predominant eschatological view in most evangelical churches at this time was that the world was getting darker and darker, the Church was getting weaker and weaker, and the only solution was for Jesus to come quickly and whisk the small remnant to heaven.

But there came a new emphasis on the kingdom of God, which saw the Church as a manifestation of God's kingdom on earth, with a mandate to advance this kingdom in every sphere of life in the here and now.

In Southampton, the young congregation was energised by this radical vision. They were committed to it, ready to dedicate their lives to making it a reality, and passionately believed in the transformative power of this new approach to church life.

Chapter Three

PART OF SOMETHING BIGGER

A major feature and influence on the formation of the church was the search for a more authentic expression of church life, like the one that was seen in the book of Acts. But that seemed so far from the lived experience of most at that time.

In the early years, the church received significant support from Bryn Jones and Arthur Wallis, as well as receiving input from several other key men, such as Dave Mansell, a recognised prophet based in north London, and as has already been mentioned, Ian McCulloch. By the time the church formed, Bryn was overseeing a growing number of new churches across the United Kingdom. These were often small and meeting in homes, which in time was referred to as the Restoration movement.

This movement, initially known as the House Church Movement, sought to build on teachings explored in the various conferences organised by Arthur Wallis and David Lillie in the 1950s and 1960s, aiming to see the restoration of New Testament principles of church life and practice.

The outworking of those meetings was both theological and practical. It resulted in a developing theology of Church as seen through the eyes of believers in the New Testament, and all linked in a practical way, as it drew leaders together – none more so than Arthur Wallis and Bryn Jones, a relationship which would have a significant impact on the Southampton church.

The vision of Restoration

By the mid to late 1970s, many groups across the United Kingdom were forming and committing to the vision of 'Restoration'.

The Restoration movement aimed to recreate the simplicity, community, and spiritual dynamism of the early Church as described in the New Testament. This included a focus on the role of apostles, prophets, evangelists, pastors and teachers as foundational for the Church (Ephesians 4:11-13). There was also a strong emphasis on the Bible as the final authority in all matters of faith and practice, rather than Church tradition, which was seen as limiting and restrictive.

The vision of returning to New Testament Christianity involved a radical rethinking of church structures and practices. Traditional hierarchies were often set aside in favour of a more egalitarian approach, reflecting the early Church's practices.

This meant that leadership was not confined to a select few but distributed among those recognised for their spiritual gifts and callings. House churches, where believers gathered in homes rather than traditional church buildings, became a hallmark of the movement. These settings were seen as more conducive to fostering intimate fellowship, mutual accountability and active participation by all members.

Spiritual renewal and revival

A central emphasis of the early pioneers was the experience of a fresh outpouring of the Holy Spirit, where all believers were encouraged to seek the baptism in the Holy Spirit, evidenced by speaking in tongues and other spiritual gifts. There was also a commitment to embracing spontaneous, Spirit-led worship, including contemporary worship music, prophetic words and gifts of the Spirit.

This desire for spiritual renewal was fuelled by a longing to see revival, such as the historical revivals in Wales in the early twentieth century and more recently in the early 1950s in the Hebrides. The Hebridean revival had significantly impacted Arthur Wallis, who had travelled there not long after the revival finished. His experiences fed into his first and possibly most far-reaching book, *In the Day of Thy Power*.[2]

The movement sought not just personal spiritual experiences but a widespread transformation that would impact communities and nations. The expectation was that as believers experienced a deeper work of the Holy Spirit, there would be visible manifestations of God's power through miracles, healings and other supernatural events. This, in turn, would draw others to Christ and spark a broader revival.

Authentic Christian community

The movement emphasised the importance of living out a genuine, everyday Christian faith in close-knit communities. Many of the groups were meeting in homes to foster deeper relationships and mutual accountability, reflecting the early Church's practices. This approach was a radical departure from the traditional expectation that 'services' should be conducted in a church building by an authorised minister.

In these house churches, members shared their lives, resources and time with one another, embodying the 'one another' commands of the New Testament. This was not just about attending meetings but about integrating faith into daily life, supporting one another in practical ways and building a sense of family and community. The goal was to create a countercultural alternative to the isolation and individualism often found in society.

Church unity

Restorationists sought to break down denominational barriers and promote unity among believers, encouraging cooperation and fellowship across denominational lines, recognising the universal body of Christ. At the same time, they advocated for the restoration of biblical church structures, including a plurality of elders and the five-fold ministry (Ephesians 4:11).

This emphasis on unity did not mean uniformity but rather a recognition of the diversity within the body of Christ. Different expressions and traditions were seen as enriching the whole. However, there was also a call for reform and renewal within existing denominations, challenging traditions and practices that were seen as unbiblical and outdated. The movement sought to bring fresh life and vitality to the whole Church, regardless of denominational affiliation.

Mission and evangelism

A strong missional focus was central to the movement's vision, prioritising evangelism and church planting, both locally and globally, and engaging in social justice and community service as expressions of the gospel in action. The movement believed that the Church was called not just to gather but to go out and 'make disciples' (Matthew 28:19), impacting society with the love and message of Christ.

This missional focus involved a holistic approach, addressing both spiritual and physical needs. Church planting was not just about establishing new congregations but about transforming communities through acts of service, advocacy for justice, and practical help for those in need. The gospel was seen as good news for the whole person and the whole of society, calling for a comprehensive engagement with the world.

Theological and practical emphases

The Restoration movement emphasised several theological and practical aspects. Kingdom theology viewed the Church as a manifestation of God's kingdom on earth, with a mandate to advance this kingdom in every sphere of life. This involved not just personal salvation but societal transformation, reflecting God's justice, peace and righteousness.

Encouraging the active use of all spiritual gifts within the Church, as outlined in 1 Corinthians 12–14, the movement believed that every believer had a role to play and that the gifts of the Spirit were essential for the Church's life and mission. Promoting the idea that every believer has a role to play in the Church's ministry, countering the traditional clergy-laity divide, meant empowering all members to use their gifts and contribute to the life and mission of the Church.

The message of the Restoration movement was reinforced and propagated through several ways, namely Bible Weeks, magazines and the new songs that were being written and sung. These methods played a crucial role in shaping the movement's identity, spreading its theological and practical emphases, and fostering a sense of community among those who were 'buying in'.

Bible Weeks

Bible Weeks were pivotal events where, by the end of the 1970s, many thousands of believers gathered for teaching, worship and fellowship. One of the precursors to the Bible Weeks associated with this new movement was an annual week-long event called the Abinger Festival held in the grounds of the Elim Bible College in Capel, Surrey. The organiser of the event, Fred Pride, an ex-Plymouth Brethren leader who had been baptised in the Holy Spirit, began to invite pioneers of what would become the Restoration movement to minister at the event. Arthur Wallis, Campbell McAlpine, American prophetess Jean Darnall, Cecil Cousens and others had all been ministering at the festival from the early 1970s.

In 1974, a new organising committee was formed, and a new name was given to the event – the Capel Bible Week. Many of those organising the event who would go on to become leaders of the new church streams – Barney Coombs, a Baptist pastor based in Basingstoke who would form the Salt and Light network, Gerald Coates, the founder of the Pioneer network, John Noble, whose Team Spirit network merged with Pioneer in the mid-nineties, and Terry Virgo, founder of Newfrontiers – were now involved.

It was decided to invite Bryn Jones and a Canadian minister, Ern Baxter, to be the main speakers in 1974. This event proved to be a significant turning point in the development of the Restoration movement as it brought together many who up to this point had been operating independently.

A second Capel Bible Week was organised in 1975 by the committee, now chaired by Mike Pusey, a charismatic-Baptist pastor from Farnham. It was agreed that Bryn Jones would organise a separate event in Wigton, Cumbria, a few weeks later, that would be called the Lakes Bible Week. This was because not many from the north of England had travelled south to Capel the previous year. Again, Ern Baxter was the main speaker at both events. The final Capel Bible Week took place in 1976. In the same year, the relocated northern Bible

Week at the Harrogate Showground, renamed the Dales Bible Week, took place for the first time.

By the end of the decade, the Dales Bible Week was attracting more than 5,000 people, with spin-off events in the north-east, south-east, south-west, Wales, Norfolk and Scotland attracting many more thousands.

These gatherings served several important functions. Well-known leaders and teachers provided in-depth teaching on Restorationist principles, the work of the Holy Spirit, spiritual gifts and New Testament Church practices. The programmes included a multitude of workshops and seminars on how to implement the teachings in local church settings.

Bible Weeks also fostered a sense of unity among believers from different regions and backgrounds, reinforcing the movement's emphasis on Christian community. Those who attended could connect with like-minded individuals, fostering relationships and collaborations that strengthened the movement's networks.

Extended times of worship and ministry allowed attendees to experience the presence of God, receive prayer and participate in prophetic ministry, reinforcing the charismatic dimension of the movement. Testimonies and prophetic words shared during these gatherings encouraged and inspired participants to pursue the vision of Restoration in their own contexts.

One of the first Bible Weeks that the members of Southampton Christian Fellowship attended was the Dales Bible Week in 1977. A report in the September 1977 edition of *Restoration*

Magazine from the Dales Bible Week gives a flavour of what was being experienced by those in attendance.

Angelic days

The BBC reported the evacuation of whole campsites in Yorkshire because of flooding during our first night in the Dales yet we had experienced the merest sprinkling of rain.

God was pleased to confirm the preaching about his angelic armies by manifesting their presence to numerous individuals throughout the week. At least 30 different persons reported choral singing in the small hours of the night. Local newspapers such as *The Telegraph* and *The Argus* carried reports of UFO sightings as glowing lights and fiery flames throughout the area that week. One 6-year-old boy lost at 11:30pm one night turned up to anxious parents at the cafeteria and brightly announced that he had been frightened but a 'nice ghost' had taken him by the hand and then vanished. Teresa Parris, 14, witnessed angelic beings dancing outside her tent at about 2:00am in the morning and wasn't sure whether to be thrilled or afraid. On returning inside she was aware of the glowing light of their presence.

Over 4500 adults gathered in the Flower Show building morning and evening in addition to the teenagers and children meeting in other places around the Great Yorkshire Showground. They responded to God's presence in a variety of ways ranging from resounding praise to awesome hush, including grand applause and rapt attention to the Word of God.

Bryn Jones pointed out the implications of the violent wind and the tongues of fire that launched this age of God's vindication of Christ's work on the cross, his declaration of intent to personally establish the rule of his Son upon earth, the eagerness of the Spirit coming with the element of violence to burn down enemy strongholds, the glorious freedom of the Spirit and the means of the word of faith as a tongue of fire.

Peter Parris and Dave Mansell added their support calling us to become what we are in Christ and let Christ be to us what he is in all his sovereign ability.

Perhaps the two highlights of the week were Ern Baxter's series on Spiritual Maturity and Bryn Jones' unforgettable teaching on Godly Family Life. Ern's themes ranged from the necessity of embracing the disciplines of life which develop Christian character and enable God to build his purpose into us, to the need to understand our inheritance in God, so we can enter a maturity which will have the impact on the world God intended.

In Bryn's first ministry on family life, he pointed out that the family is the unit upon which God builds his Church. The Church will only be as strong as the families that make it up. This principle was brought home as Bryn shared how God had dealt with him personally in order that he might reflect more of God's fatherly nature to his children. Bryn's closing message on the last night will be remembered for a long time as we were left with a powerful impression of the dignity and stature God has given us in Christ to be overcomers in every situation.

Magazines

Magazines, and in particular *Restoration Magazine*, were vital tools for disseminating the message of Restoration. Edited initially by Bryn Jones, the magazine provided theological articles, news and updates, promoting unity and the shared vision of the movement. It also offered practical advice on church planting, discipleship, and leadership development.

Its stated purpose as printed in the editorial of each magazine was communicated in this way:

> The name Restoration expresses our conviction that the Spirit of God is moving within the church today not merely to renew what exists but to restore so much that has been lost or neglected. This work of the Spirit is a prophetic fulfilment of the Scripture concerning Christ, 'whom heaven must receive until the time of restoration of all things which God has spoken by the mouth of all his holy prophets since the world began', Acts chapter 2 verse 21. The teaching articles deal with issues about which the Holy Spirit is speaking in the Church today to bring us all to the perfection God desires as seen in our Lord Jesus Christ.

Restoration Magazine was published quarterly for more than twenty years, providing articles and updates on events happening around the UK and the world. It also gave opportunities for the leaders to write extended articles on subjects that were relevant to the Church at the time. It was one of the main tools for promoting the values and beliefs of the movement. The magazine provided a platform for theological reflection, practical teaching and testimonies from various churches and individuals involved in the movement.

The articles covered a wide range of topics, from theological discussions on the nature of the Church and the role of spiritual gifts to practical advice on church leadership, community life and evangelism. The magazine also featured reports from various conferences, Bible Weeks and other events, helping to connect and inform those involved in the movement.

Examples of the magazine content included in-depth discussions on key Restorationist principles, such as the role of apostles and prophets, and the importance of spiritual gifts. These articles provided a theological foundation for the movement and helped shape its beliefs and practices.

There were articles offering practical advice on various aspects of church life, such as how to lead a house church, how to disciple new believers and how to engage in effective evangelism, providing practical tools and strategies for those involved in church leadership and ministry.

Stories and testimonies from individuals and churches involved in the movement provided experience and insight, serving to encourage and inspire others and helping to build a sense of community and shared purpose. Additionally, reports on various events and developments within the movement, such as upcoming conferences, new church plants, and notable achievements, kept the movement connected and informed, fostering a sense of unity and shared vision.

New songs

New songs also played a significant role in the movement, both in worship expression and in reinforcing its message. Southampton Christian Fellowship had a wealth of songwriters that were producing new songs almost on a weekly basis.

Songs written by members, such as Dilly Fung, Carolyn Govier, Wendy Churchill, Sue Hutchinson, Dave Evans, Alan Matlock and others, were published and sung across the nation.

The first printed song book was produced by the church in 1976 and was titled *Unto Him*. It contained just over 100 songs divided into four sections – praise, the body, worship and devotion.

Here are the titles of some of the songs that were being written and sung at that time:

> Jesus is Lord! Creation's Voice Proclaims It
> Therefore The Redeemed Of The Lord Shall Return
> I've Taken My Harp Down
> We Are Gathering Together Unto Him
> Jesus Stand Among Us
> Great Things
> For I'm Building A People of Power

The new songs being written in Southampton and other places contributed to the movement in several ways. Theologically, the songs often contained lyrics that reflected the movement's emphases, embedding its beliefs and values in the hearts and minds of those who sang them. These songs reinforced key theological concepts such as the centrality of Christ, the power of the Holy Spirit and the importance of the Church as a community of believers.

In terms of worship and spiritual renewal, the new songs encouraged active participation in worship, fostering an atmosphere of spiritual renewal and engagement. The contemporary style and heartfelt lyrics resonated with many believers, helping to create a worship experience that was both vibrant and meaningful.

The shared repertoire of songs helped to unify the movement, creating a sense of shared identity and purpose. These songs were sung at various gatherings, Bible Weeks and church meetings, fostering a sense of connection and solidarity among those involved in the movement.

Furthermore, the new songs often expressed the vision and values of the Restoration movement, such as the desire for revival, the call to mission and the commitment to community. The songs served as a powerful means of expressing and communicating the movement's vision, helping to inspire and mobilise those involved.

The impact on Southampton

For the young congregation in Southampton, these elements of the Restoration movement created an intoxicating environment. Gathering with thousands of like-minded individuals from across the nation at events like the Dales Bible Week was a transformative experience. The inspiring prophetic preaching, enthusiastic worship and communal living around campfires and shared meals all added to the sense of being part of a special move of God.

The congregation's involvement in the movement meant that they were constantly exposed to fresh theological insights and practical teachings that helped shape their community life and whole identity, with an increased sense of mission. The songs they sang, the articles they read and the gatherings they attended all reinforced a shared vision and identity, which was crucial in maintaining momentum and growth.

Chapter Four

Tony Morton

Back in the autumn of 1968, Tony Morton, a young college student, found himself in a state of profound despair. Deeply immersed in existential philosophy, he had come to the bleak conclusion that life was devoid of meaning, and had even contemplated suicide. Seeking solace, he wandered into Liverpool's Protestant cathedral, a magnificent edifice known for its towering spires and majestic stained-glass windows.

As he entered the Chapel of the Holy Spirit, the sun cast a radiant beam through the window depicting Christ praying in the garden of Gethsemane. This ethereal moment was a turning point for Tony. Suddenly, he became acutely aware of an inner voice speaking to him, saying,

'He died for you, just live for him.'

This divine encounter filled Tony with an overwhelming sense of peace. He walked out of the cathedral transformed, though he had no knowledge of Christianity or its community.

Embracing a new path

Following this profound experience, Tony decided to leave the business college he had enrolled at in London. Instead, he took up a volunteer role in Liverpool, caring for children with complex special needs. This marked the beginning of his new path, one that would be characterised by service and spiritual growth.

In the autumn of 1969, Tony started a language degree course at the University of Southampton. On only his second day, he met an evangelical Christian who handed him a tract and told him that he needed to be 'born again'. Though unfamiliar with Christian terminology, Tony realised that what the stranger was describing mirrored his own recent experience.

Tony began attending Above Bar Church, an evangelical church in the city pastored by Dr Leith Samuel. Despite his active participation in evangelism, Tony saw little success in his efforts. He felt a deep need for greater fruitfulness in his witness and an extra dimension of power in his life to lead people to Jesus and to overcome his own struggles with sin.

During this period, Tony encountered Pentecostals who told him that he needed to be filled with the Holy Spirit. Initially, he rejected this idea as unbiblical. However, after a time of soul-searching, Tony realised that this might be what he needed. In a moment of desperation, he prayed, 'Lord, I don't know what the terms are, and I don't actually want to be filled with the Holy Spirit but come and do whatever needs to be done to me so that I can really live this life for you.'

Tony experienced a dramatic infilling of the Holy Spirit, although he did not speak in tongues at that moment. A few months later, he prayed for the gift of tongues and immediately began speaking in a new heavenly language.

After his second year at university, Tony spent a year in Spain as part of his language course. He took a teaching job in Madrid to support himself but spent every spare moment evangelising. In the early 1970s, Spain was a challenging place for evangelism due to restrictions on open-air preaching. This experience deepened Tony's commitment to missionary work and left a lasting impression on his life and ministry.

Upon returning to Southampton, Tony found an increased opposition within the university Christian Union to the charismatic experience. He eventually joined the group of students who were hungry for more of the Spirit at the Saturday afternoon Agape Fellowship, where he quickly emerged as a key leader.

Early ministry and leadership

When Tony's course finished in 1973, he took a job in advertising in Teddington, south-west London. He was dating a girl from university, Hannah, who would later become his wife, and he continued to be part of the leadership of the Agape Fellowship, travelling to Southampton every weekend. During this time, he met two men who would become influential figures in his life, Bryn Jones and Arthur Wallis.

Tony felt a strong call from God to full-time Christian ministry. A significant confirmation came through Isaiah 37:30, which states:

This will be a sign for you . . . 'This year you will eat what grows by itself, and the second year what springs from that. But in the third year sow and reap, plant vineyards, and eat their fruit.'

Tony's journey mirrored this scripture. He worked in advertising for a year, then moved to a new role in another company the next year. At the end of the second year, he married Hannah, and they set up home in Southampton, spending the following year at a teacher training college in the city.

Growth of the church

By this time, the new church, Southampton Christian Fellowship, had outgrown its initial meeting place at the Centre for the Blind and had moved to The Gregg School in Winn Road. Bryn had appointed Tony as the main leader in 1976, and in 1977, when the church merged with West End Evangelical Church, Tony began to co-lead the newly formed Southampton Community Church with Bob Hall, leader of the West End Evangelical Church.

Arthur Wallis, who had been overseeing the church in West End, became a mentor to Tony. Arthur's integrity and ability to equip others provided stability for the new fellowship and for Tony personally.

After about a year, Bob Hall stepped down, leaving Tony with full leadership responsibility. Tony was now working for and being paid by the church in his role as leader, and four elders had been appointed by Bryn to work alongside him.

Tony was eager to grow in his leadership and was hungry to learn. For one so young he had an ability to articulate deep spiritual truths simply and with relevance. He had a clear vision for what God wanted to do in the city and beyond, and communicated with warmth and with unique Liverpudlian humour.

Expanding the ministry

Tony's apostolic gift soon became evident. Isaiah's prophecy continued to unfold as groups from across the region began attending meetings in Southampton. Tony and his team started establishing new churches, beginning in Gosport, and extending to Hedge End, Eastleigh, Romsey, Winchester, Andover and Totton.

Over the next few years, celebration evenings at Southampton Guildhall became a regular fixture. These events, hosted three or four times a year, at the largest venue in the city, were attracting around 1,000 people from across the city and region. The worship was led by musicians from the church, and the evenings featured various speakers from across the United Kingdom and further afield.

Tony's ministry and what was happening across the city gained wider recognition, and this growing interest led to the organisation of a non-residential Bible Week in July 1978 with speakers Bob Mumford, an associate of Ern Baxter based in the USA, and Dave Mansell.

In 1980, the first New Forest Bible Week was hosted at New Park in Brockenhurst, attracting more than 800 attendees. The organising team was led by Ken Ford, leader of the group now meeting in Totton. Subsequent Bible Weeks in the summers of 1981 and 1982 saw even greater participation. Having outgrown the site in Brockenhurst, the Bible Week event moved to the Royal South and West Showground at Shepton Mallet in Somerset in 1983.

The church appointed Pete and Dilly Fung as leaders of the growing number of musicians and singers, and the church worship team released the first cassette tape of new songs in 1978, titled *The Lord Reigns* with eighteen new songs, and another, *More Than Life*, in 1981, featuring fourteen new songs also written by church members, including 'O Lord Most Holy God', 'Our Eyes Have Seen the King' and 'Jesus is King and I Will Enthrone Him'.

This was followed by three worship albums recorded at the South & West Bible Weeks, *Let His Praise be Heard*, *Sing a New Psalm* and *Let the Righteous be Glad*, all produced by Kingsway Music.

International outreach and training

Tony's ministry also extended internationally. He travelled to India and Nepal with Alan Vincent and visited churches in Argentina with Arthur Wallis. He travelled with Dave Adcock, Peter Light and Geoff Wright on a scouting trip to four cities in France and began to develop links with churches in Belgium and London.

Tony had now joined Bryn Jones' apostolic team and would travel to Bradford regularly for team meetings. His visits to Bradford also enabled him to spend time with Arthur and Eileen Wallis and his good friend, Martyn Dunsford.

In 1980, Tony proposed that the church establish a full-time training programme called Foundations for Ministry to equip emerging leaders across the church. One of the elders, Roger Popplestone, was given the task of developing the programme.

As the church continued to grow, it outgrew yet another school hall, leading to the decision to meet in four area settings with a monthly celebration at the University of Southampton's Boldrewood lecture theatre. This arrangement allowed Tony to operate more 'apostolically' and provided opportunities for new leaders to emerge within the area settings.

Community Impact

The area settings – Bitterne, Highfield, Shirley and Hollybrook – provided a conducive environment for discipleship, community development and local outreach. The larger monthly celebrations at Boldrewood offered the opportunity for dynamic worship, prophetic teaching and prayer ministry.

There were also about twenty home groups now operating across the city, from Bitterne on the east, across to St Denys, to Pointout and Upper Shirley on the west. These were places where relationships could be nurtured and community formed.

In addition, regular Bible studies were organised at the church building in West End, with key leaders and elders leading Bible surveys and character studies.

Communication was a key priority for the leadership in these early years as many new people were joining and becoming a part of the growing church. The weekly news-sheet was available at each of the area settings with details of upcoming events and news. Each month, the *Agape Magazine*, edited by Jean Brand, covered more comprehensively all that was going on across the church and regular 'fireside chats' in each of the area settings providing an opportunity for elders and leaders to share updates and receive feedback from members.

During this period, Dave Adcock emerged as a key leader. Captured by his first experience at the Centre for the Blind, Dave very quickly began hosting Sunday meetings and, in early 1981, left his teaching job to work full-time for the church, focusing on young people, students and outreach.

A key theme of the church's message was the kingdom of God influencing every area of life. This inspired several church members to integrate their faith with their professional lives, leading to innovative initiatives in medicine, education and business.

Medicine

Two recently qualified doctors, Phil Clarke and Barry Trewinnard, had a vision for a holistic approach to General Practice. A practice that would be fully Christian, offering an excellent standard of medical care while looking at the needs of the whole person in terms of body, soul and spirit.

They decided to set up a practice in one of the more deprived housing estates in the city that was 'under-doctored'. This was a huge financial risk as doctors only got paid if they had adequate patient numbers and, in those days, they were not allowed to advertise. To help the project get up and running, everyone in the church at that time was encouraged to sign up as patients!

They leased a unit in a parade of shops on the estate and opened the surgery in September 1981. By the end of the year, they had 199 patients. This wasn't quite enough for both doctors to get paid, so Phil and Barry worked other jobs in the NHS to supplement their income.

Numbers grew steadily and within three years they had just over 1,400 patients. The opportunity to take over another surgery that operated on another housing estate became a possibility and, after much negotiation (and prayer), Phil and Barry became the partners of that surgery with its additional 4,500 patients.

The King's School

Education became a major focus for the church. As more members started families, they questioned the suitability of the secular education system for their children. This led to the establishment of The King's School, offering a Christian education that integrated faith with academic learning.

Paul Trevett, who up to this point coordinated children's work across the church and was a secondary school teacher, was commissioned to explore this possibility. After researching various educational models, the eldership chose the

Accelerated Christian Education (ACE) programme from America, which emphasised individualised learning with a Christian worldview. This model was already being used by a newly formed school in Basingstoke, which offered great support and advice.

The West End church building, an underused asset, was chosen as the school's location. Geoff Wright, one of the eldership team became the headteacher, with Paul Trevett working alongside him, and The King's School launched in September 1982, providing a Christian education to thirty-seven children from twenty families from the church community.

Business development

A group of business professionals in the church formed a kingdom business group to support each other in integrating their faith with their work. This initiative fostered a network of Christian businesses, from builders to financial advisors to retailers, committed to ethical practices and community impact.

This eclectic group would meet on a regular basis to pray for each other and their business, support each other as they faced difficulties and challenges and celebrate their success together.

Cornerstone

In late 1981, at a conference in Ilkley, Tony was released from Bryn's apostolic team to form his own team serving the south and south-west of England. Cornerstone, an apostolic team and network of churches, was born. The original team included Peter Light, Arthur Wallis, David Damp, a pioneer church leader from Gosport, and Tony.

This marked the beginning of a new season in the life of the church. Tony's leadership and vision continued to inspire and guide the church community, impacting countless lives locally, as well as developing strategies for church planting and mission across the south of England and internationally.

Restoration Magazine, March 1981

growing churches

THE COMMUNITY CHURCH, SOUTHAMPTON

'For the vision is yet for an appointed time – though it tarry, wait for it; it will certainly come, it will not delay' (Hab 2:3).

Now four years old, with about five hundred committed members and supporting several full-time ministers, the Community Church in Southampton can trace its roots back to a move of God in the early 1970's. At that time many local Christians in all denominations were blessed with the baptism of the Holy Spirit and along with this refreshing came a hunger to grow in the Lord and see him glorified through his church in the city. God laid a burden of intercession on the hearts of many to see the Holy Spirit moving in might among a people living in the reality of Christ's resurrection power.

In the university a number of students began to meet together, initially to pray for the work on campus, but God extended the burden to pray for revival through the university to the city and even to the world beyond. As they prayed God began to unfold by stages the things he expected of them in individual commitment, in worship and in community life. As they received his word and reached to him for the faith to walk in it, so he prepared their hearts for the next step in his unfolding plan. A communal tea, 'The Agape', developed into a time for prayer and worship, and later for teaching too as God raised up leaders to share his heart. As the believers learned to submit to the Lordship of Christ in every area of their lives, they were prepared for teaching on spiritual authority and church government – a step that then enabled this amorphous group of students to find a common bond with two housegroups which had grown up in the city. Under the direction of Bryn Jones and Dave Mansell, the three groups came together as the Southampton Christian Fellowship.

At that time it was thrilling to see how God had been preparing and leading the three separate groups so similarly towards this union, and the first meeting in March 1975 saw about 60 people gathering with much excitement to worship God together. The greatness of God's love and the importance of right relationships were the major emphasis. Although at first there was very little numerical growth, God was laying a groundwork of commitment, body ministry and worship which was to be very important in the days of expansion ahead. Sunday meetings were first held in a Day Centre for the Blind and then in school halls. The weekday meetings continued in small housegroups, with the university group of about forty soon dividing down into more workable units.

By 1976 the leaders were in close contact with those of an Evangelical church at West End, on the outskirts of the city, which was being covered by Arthur Wallis. In October '77 the two churches joined under the new name, The Community Church. Arthur and Dave Mansell came to set in elders and encourage the church to move forward in unity and faith. Since then Arthur has had a continuing ministry of covering and input to the church, thereby strengthening relationships with what God is doing in many other parts of the country.

Growth continued and accelerated. By the end of 1978 the church had to leave the school hall because numbers exceeded those allowed by fire regulations. Since then, despite continual prayer and much careful searching, no suitable venues have been found for regular Sunday worship for the whole body. It was a good discipline for a time to be deprived of dependence on big meetings. The lack of a hall emphasised the importance of each individual's commitment and ministry and there was much growth within the smaller groups based in homes.

A time of worship in one of the monthly church meetings, held in a large lecture theatre at the University.

By this time the leaders of the church were having more and more contact with groups outside Southampton and several fellowships developed under the oversight of Tony Morton. It has been thrilling to see God's purposes in restoration extending out beyond local boundaries and to know a oneness in him with those he is leading along similar paths in different places.

As an interim measure, monthly church meetings were begun on Saturday evenings in a large lecture theatre at the university. God has greatly used these times and they gave opportunity for the church to be exposed to those outside. Many who have come to watch have been converted, healed, filled with the Spirit and found themselves challenged by God to commit themselves fully to him. As God continued to close doors in the search for a suitable hall, the elders began to feel he was preparing us for a new stage in our ministry. Since last September the church has been meeting on Sundays in four area settings, so allowing families with children to come and worship together. This also facilitates the children's work and allows a more local base for outreach in the different parts of the city. The monthly evening meeting has been retained, thus keeping a sense of 'one body' and the vision for the city.

From the church's inception God laid a burden on hearts to pray for a great move of his Spirit in Southampton. Now, with an established church structure, five elders, twenty housegroups and an effective administration, God is stressing that the church is at a new place of beginning. He has been teaching believers to live individually each day in the power of the Holy Spirit, to deepen unity by serving one another in faith, and as a body to move out in spiritual warfare to pull down the strongholds of Satan in our city and to set the captives free.

The vision, of course, goes beyond Southampton. The leaders are looking to God to use the church as a base for reaching out to many different areas, bringing the gospel of the kingdom as he has revealed it in their own area. In the future the church expects to send out teams of trained ministers and believe that many lands will be touched from this centre. At the Bible Week God called the church to a place of priestly intercession to bring into being the revelation he has given (Ps 2:8).

Though the work has progressed so far, God is constantly stressing that he has so much more for his people as they look to see the kingdom extended throughout the earth.

> 'Look at the nations and watch and be utterly amazed.
> For I am going to do something in your days that you would not believe even if you were told' (Hab 1:5).

The Leaders

At present there is a leadership team of five elders, led by Tony Morton. Although the elders work very much as a team, each has his own sphere of responsibility and there is also a full-time administrator whose job it is to ensure eldership decisions are implemented and all runs as smoothly as possible.

Tony and Hannah Morton came to Southampton as students and have been involved in the church from the very beginning. After graduating, Tony worked for a time in advertising and then, with Hannah, trained for teaching. After a very hectic year as teachers, also coping with the demands of shepherding and teaching in the growing fellowship, they moved into full-time ministry in 1976.

Tony's ministry now extends well beyond the confines of Southampton. For some years he has been involved in establishing and strengthening other fellowships in Hampshire and one in Teddington, and as the eldership has developed Tony has been more free to give of himself in leadership training, both here and overseas.

Chris Thomas

Chris Thomas, one of the original student group at Southampton University, now edits Agape, the church magazine. Her husband, Adrian, is a deacon.

The elders meet every Monday for a day of prayer and fellowship. The picture shows, from left to right, the full time elders: Tony Morton, Geoff Wright, Roger Popplestone and Peter Light. The other elder, not shown, is Mick Caws.

Chapter Five

Finding My Feet

I arrived in Southampton in May 1982. I had just turned twenty years old. I was a manager with the sports retailer Olympus Sport, and had been invited to move to Southampton to take over the management of the store in Above Bar Street.

I had been on my own spiritual journey since leaving home three years previously to pursue my career in retail management. My journey had taken me from my first post in Glasgow to Belfast to Liverpool to Cardiff, Bromley and now Southampton.

I had been raised in a very conservative non-charismatic evangelical church with parents who were the 'real deal'. They lived what they believed. They had a deep love for God and a trust in him for everything, no matter how small or trivial.

As I travelled from city to city, I wanted to explore what other churches did. I remember visiting a rather scary Pentecostal church in Belfast where we were all encouraged to raise our arms in worship. I just couldn't do it. And then at City Temple in Cardiff I heard someone speak in tongues for the first time. Although this made me feel anxious it was something that I was curious about and I wanted to know more.

Following a move to Bromley for my work, I decided to spend the weekends at the home of my aunt and uncle, Dot and Andy Croall, in Beaconsfield, Buckinghamshire. They were part of a Baptist church that had experienced charismatic renewal and had been exposed to Restoration teaching. The church had a vibrant youth and young adult group that were on fire for God. I was so glad to find this group, but still had a lot of questions that sprang from my non-, or more accurately, anti-charismatic upbringing.

Starting out

When I announced that I had been invited to go and manage the store in Southampton, my aunt enthusiastically produced the March 1981 edition of *Restoration Magazine* which featured the story of the Southampton Community Church. I agreed to check them out.

Back in those days there was no Google and no such thing as internet searches. We had to rely on the phone book for addresses and telephone numbers. The address in the telephone book for Southampton Community Church was Quob Lane, West End, Southampton.

Again, these were the days before GPS or the Sat Nav so I drove my Vauxhall Chevette to the west end of Southampton hoping someone could direct me to Quob Lane. Eventually,

I stopped someone who advised me that West End was in the eastern part of the city.

I made my way across town and eventually found the building, but unfortunately it was shut!

There was a board outside that listed three names with telephone numbers. I made my way to the nearest telephone box, conveniently situated at the end of Quob Lane, and called the numbers on the board.

I rang the first one. No reply.

The second one. No reply.

The third one. Someone answered.

'Hi,' I said. 'My name is Billy and I'm trying to find Southampton Community Church.'

'Where are you?' the person replied.

'I'm in the phone box at the end of Quob Lane,' I said.

'Wait there. I'll be five minutes,' came the response.

I later learned that Mervyn had been in the garden watering the flowers and Joan, his wife, was getting anxious because it was time to leave for the church meeting. But Mervyn had a sense that he should wait and not rush. He said he felt it was a Holy Spirit prompting.

And, five minutes later, I had rung.

Mervyn and Joan came to the phone box and directed me to follow them. We drove from West End towards town, through

Bitterne and turned into Midanbury Lane and from there into Beech Avenue and the grounds of Beechwood Junior School where the meeting was being held.

The meeting had already started. I knew that even before I walked in as I could hear the singing in the entrance area. When I entered the hall, I was amazed to see about 120 people, all worshipping enthusiastically, led by two or three musicians on guitars, a young teenager operating the overhead projector, with the majority of the congregation from the youngest to the oldest dancing, moving, arms raised, with joy on their faces.

It was incredible. I'd not seen the like of it before. Such joy in the singing, such freedom in the worship.

But as much as I enjoyed what I was witnessing, I felt somewhat detached and separate from it.

Mervyn and Joan asked me back for lunch, to which I happily agreed. We chatted about the church, my job, my family, their journey, football and anything else that came up. I learned that Mervyn and Joan had been a part of the West End Evangelical Church that had merged to form the Southampton Community Church. He had been one of the elders in the church and had a real passion for God. He ran his own business selling office equipment, which kept him busy. After lunch Mervyn asked if I'd like to attend a home group meeting that week. I didn't know what a home group was but agreed anyway.

On Wednesday evening I turned up at the home of Rob and Heather. Mike and Jane were already there along with Jeff and Liz, Mick and Sue and 'tall' Paul. Mervyn and Joan turned up and the meeting began. Even though there were only a handful of people, the worship was amazing, but for me somewhat scary. I had been warned by others that in this type of environment people could go into trances and be exposed to demonic forces. I had my head in my hands. At this point, someone said, 'I believe there is someone in the room that has a problem with the Holy Spirit and spiritual gifts.'

I thought, 'How do they know that?'

Looking back now it was obvious that I was struggling, and I declared, 'That's me.' I explained my hang-ups and the thoughts that were running through my head. They very graciously listened to my concerns and then offered to pray for me to be filled with the Holy Spirit.

Nothing happened.

I was glad in one way. Maybe what I had been taught in my non-charismatic church was right. But the other part of me was disappointed. I so wanted what I'd seen in the church in Beaconsfield and now in this group of people in Southampton.

As the meeting was closing someone asked if they could say something.

They had a 'word'.

For me!

I can't remember the exact words, but it was along the lines that God had called me to leadership and more specifically to leadership in this church. And some of those sitting in that front room that evening would one day look to me for leadership.

I'd never heard a prophetic word before and didn't quite know what to make of it – or if I would ever return to the church again!

The next day everything changed.

All change

I was sitting in my car waiting for someone. As I sat there, I began to hum one of the tunes I had heard at church on the previous Sunday morning. As I hummed, I sensed the car fill with what I can only describe as the presence of God. That presence then seemed to envelop me and go deep down to the core of my being. My humming turned to words, words that I didn't understand, a heavenly language, and from deep inside there was an explosion of joy.

In that split second, all that I had learned about the love of God and the victory of Christ's death on the cross moved from my head to my heart. I knew in that moment that my sins had been forgiven, my slate had been wiped clean. I was loved by the Father and he had a purpose and destiny for me.

I had been baptised in the Holy Spirit.

For me it was like being born again, again.

I couldn't wait for the next meeting. I was devouring the Scriptures. Any free time I had would be devoted to prayer and worship. I was hungry to learn more. I had no hesitation sharing with my friends, talking about Jesus, praying for people. This is what I'd been searching for.

That summer I attended the Downs Bible Week with my friends from Beaconsfield. I remember being deeply impacted by Alan Vincent and Terry Virgo as well as a young Dave Holden. But it was the worship that was the highlight. One song stands out. The lyrics were along the lines of getting so excited when we realise we are forgiven. I really couldn't contain my excitement when this song started up. By the end of the week my throat was hoarse with singing and shouting, and my whole body was tired with dancing.

I returned to Southampton just in time for the final night of the New Forest Bible Week in Brockenhurst. Bryn Jones was speaking. I can't remember what he spoke about, but I still remember the atmosphere in that tent with 2,000 other people. It was the same atmosphere I had experienced at the Downs Bible Week at Plumpton Racecourse the previous week. There was something happening that I now felt on the inside of rather than the feeling of detachment and separation I felt when I first arrived in town.

As is the case with most churches, the year starts properly in September in line with the academic year. That same September, 1982, after many months of planning, The King's School began at the West End building. The church hosted one of its regular evening celebrations at Southampton Guildhall to kick off the year and I started Firm Foundations.

Firm Foundations

Firm Foundations was a six-week course that the church ran for people new to the church. I had been encouraged to sign up for the course to learn more about the church's vision and values.

The content was based on some verses at the beginning of Hebrews 6 (vv1-3):

> Therefore let us move beyond the elementary teachings about Christ and be taken forward to maturity, not laying again the foundation of repentance from acts that lead to death, and of faith in God, instruction about cleansing rites, the laying on of hands, the resurrection of the dead, and eternal judgment. And God permitting, we will do so.

Over the next six weeks we explored the key elements of the church's developed vision.

The first session covered 'repentance and faith' where we looked at the need to move away from dead religious ritual as well as sin. I'd not really come across the repentance from dead works before, but I recognised it in my life.

Again, I encountered a new element to the subject of faith. Faith that was more than faith in Christ's work of salvation but a whole life of faith where we were dependent on God for everything.

The second session covered 'baptism' and included both water baptism and the baptism in the Holy Spirit. Many were joining the church who may have been baptised as children in a more traditional church and many were re-baptised by full immersion (often to the annoyance of parents and former clergy). What was emphasised in this session was the nature of being baptised into a body, a group of people that we were now called to share life with.

Which led to session three where we looked at 'fellowship' that focused on both fellowship with Christ through prayer, Bible reading in time set aside and the importance of fellowship with our fellow believers. This was deeply practical as well as spiritual.

We then had a whole session on 'authority and submission' that included the issue of head covering referenced in 1 Corinthians 11 (we'll pick up more on this later). I later learned that the issue of 'authority and submission' had been taken to excess in some Restoration church contexts.

I had been made aware of 'green forms' that members of the church in Southampton filled out when they would meet with their 'local elder' where they would be expected to give feedback on different areas of their lives and included everything from how they were spending their money to their relationships and 'quiet times'. One former eldership couple told me that in the very early days of the church they could be out up to five nights a week seeing people and working through the 'green forms'. Thankfully, by the time I arrived the 'green forms' had been ditched as the leadership realised that this approach had led in some instances towards the 'heavy shepherding' that was being discredited in many circles.

There was a session on 'finances' where the practice of tithing was strongly encouraged as well as the exhortation to be trusting God for finances in our everyday lives.

And the final session was entitled 'Going on to Maturity' with a call to lifelong discipleship.

It was a well-crafted course setting out many of the principles that were being adopted by Restoration churches and that set out very clearly what the expectations were for those wishing to be a part of the church.

Looking back now, there was a strong call to radical discipleship that I know was challenging to some. But for me, I was in – hook, line and sinker!

In this, my first year at the church, I was getting a growing sense that there was something God was calling me into. As I read my Bible one day, God highlighted some verses to me from Isaiah 37:30:

> This will be the sign for you, Hezekiah:
> 'This year you will eat what grows by itself,
> and the second year what springs from that.
> But in the third year sow and reap,
> plant vineyards and eat their fruit.'

It was sometime later that I discovered Tony had received the exact same Scripture.

Over the next few months, I received three or four prophetic words that indicated that God was calling me to serve him in some form of church-based ministry. I was reluctant because my father had been in church ministry, and I saw the challenges of that role. Also, I was successful in my work and really enjoyed it. I had assumed that this would be my career.

I met with my group leader, Mike Evans, who offered me great support and advice. I then began to meet with Peter Light, our local elder, on a regular basis and over the course of the next few months he suggested I apply to go on the church's Foundation for Ministry course starting the following September, 1983.

I spent a long time considering this option and eventually decided this is what I would do. My plan was to enjoy this first year, eating what was growing, do the Foundation for Ministry course in the second year, which had sprung from my first year, and then, in the third year, sow, reap and plant vineyards!

Although, I had no idea what this would look like!

One unexpected and life-changing surprise that occurred during this time was meeting my future wife. Caroline had been part of the church since 1980 and shared a house with some friends in a part of the city called St Denys. The girls in the house had begun an outreach to some children in the area, and over time this grew to become a weekly children's club at the local community centre. I volunteered to help at the club (with no ulterior motives!) and developed a close friendship with Caroline. Our friendship blossomed, we got engaged in February of 1984 and married on 1st September at the end of the Foundation for Ministry course.

Our partnership produced three children, David, Erin and Daniel, and today, at the latest count, five grandchildren!

Chapter Six

WORDS, WORKS AND WONDERS

Over the next couple of years there was lots of movement and change across the church.

Movement

Roy and Gill Pearson had already moved from Bitterne Park to Hedge End and a new group was developing in that expanding village on the edge of the city with weekly Sunday meetings in the Hedge End Village Hall. Phil and Maggie Orchard also moved from Bitterne Park to Bitterne to pioneer a new home group in that part of the city. Mick and Fran Caws moved from their home in West End to take responsibility for the group that was forming in Eastleigh.

Ken Ford, who had only recently been appointed as an elder in the church, and his wife, Heather, and their family moved to lead a church in Bridgwater, that had connected through the Bible Weeks that we had been hosting. Geoff and Norah Wright moved across to Fareham to lead the newly formed

Fareham Community Church. Peter and Lesley Light moved from their home in Bitterne Park to live opposite Tony and Hannah in Pointout Road in Bassett, taking on a wider role across the Cornerstone network in addition to Pete's pastoral responsibilities in the city. He would later move to lead the church in Romsey and continue his work with Cornerstone leading the Impact Asia team, Cornerstone's ministry on that continent.

Roger and Chris Popplestone moved to London as leaders of the Teddington Christian Fellowship with a view to strengthen and develop the connections across south-west London. Roger Hutchins, who had been a student for three years at Southampton university when the Agape Fellowship formed, together with his wife, Ann, moved from the Teddington church in London to Portsmouth to pioneer a new church there and lead the Foundation of Ministry programme.

New elders were appointed to lead the area settings that had been vacated by those moving on – Dave Adcock took responsibility to lead in Hollybrook, Allan Cox in Highfield and Phil Orchard in Bitterne.

As well as those who were moving out of the city, several significant arrivals took place.

Arrivals

Arthur and Eileen Wallis, together with their son, Jonathan, his wife, Sylvia, and their family, moved from Bradford to Southampton. This was more than significant.

Arthur had been supporting the church since its inception and had built a strong relationship with Tony and the other leaders. Everyone was very excited that Arthur and Eileen would now be joining the church and using Southampton as their base for wider ministry.

They were soon followed by Martyn and Gaynor Dunsford and their family, and Colin and Brenda Henderson, also from Bradford.

Martyn had been instrumental in the formation of the Agape Fellowship in the early 1970s and had introduced Bryn Jones to the group. Martyn had moved to Bradford to work with Bryn when his university course finished and attended a local teacher training college before starting to work as a teacher. In time, Martyn took responsibility to lead the church in Bradford and oversaw a period of significant growth. But he had always felt that one day he would return to Southampton to work alongside Tony, with whom he had maintained a strong friendship.

Martyn moved down to Southampton and immediately joined the eldership team with responsibility for the groups on the east side of the city.

Colin Henderson had been a wing commander in the Royal Air Force and had spent the previous few years working at a drug rehabilitation centre in the north of England, as well as using his administrative skills to serve the church in Bradford and the growing network led by Bryn Jones.

The timing of their arrival could not have been better. The church had recently purchased a building in the city to use as an administrative centre and meeting venue. This building was on the High Street in Shirley and had been variously used as a library and police station. Now that it was owned by the church it was renamed King's House.

There was much work to do to refurbish the building and added to that, a significant increase in administration required for the growing network and annual Bible Weeks. Colin was employed as the administration manager alongside Adrian Thomas, who had recently left his job in banking. Hilary Anderson, the church administrator, and Sue Earley, the administrative assistant, completed the team.

King's House provided office space for all the administrative staff, a kitchen, small downstairs hall seating thirty, and an upstairs hall seating about 100. As well as the office, the building was used for leaders' meetings, youth meetings, prayer meetings, training seminars and was the venue for the soon to be formed Freemantle area local groups.

Direction

It was at one of the midweek leaders' gatherings where I first met and listened to Roger Forster, the leader of the Ichthus Christian Fellowship. Roger was teaching from a passage in Romans 15:17-20:

> Therefore I glory in Christ Jesus in my service to God. I will not venture to speak of anything except what Christ has accomplished through me in leading the Gentiles to obey God by what I have said and done – by the power of signs and wonders, through the power

of the Spirit of God. So from Jerusalem all the way around to Illyricum, I have fully proclaimed the gospel of Christ. It has always been my ambition to preach the gospel where Christ was not known, so that I would not be building on someone else's foundation.

The title of his talk was, 'Words, works and wonders'.

The theme deeply resonated with all of us present. The church had experienced exceptional growth up to this point, but we all recognised that most of this growth had come about through those already professing Christian faith who had come into a new experience of the Holy Spirit. Tony had a strong conviction that this type of growth was not sustainable, and we needed now to be much more focused in reaching out to those outside the walls of the church.

Roger's talk gave us the clear sense of direction that we needed to be reaching out using our words in proclamation, serving the needs of our city through our 'works' and looking to God for his supernatural intervention.

We continued to develop the area settings that enabled us to be closer to the communities that we were seeking to reach. New gatherings started in Freemantle, meeting at King's House, Townhill Park, Woolston, Lordswood and West End. And we continued with the monthly celebrations at the university's Boldrewood lecture theatre.

City impact

In March 1984, Jonathan and Sylvia Wallis organised a 'rock musical', *The Witness*, covering the life and times of Jesus, as told from the perspective of the disciple Peter. This musical by Jimmy and Carol Owens was performed by members of the church over three nights at the Mountbatten Theatre in the city centre, with an additional performance at Eastleigh's town theatre. The turnout and response at all the performances was amazing.

I was invited to form an evangelistic team that would serve the city and the growing Cornerstone network of churches. The team would begin to operate in the summer of 1984. I was tasked with recruiting some team members and invited Tony Rozee, a proven evangelist, with a background in theatre, Mike Pearson, the son of Roy and Gill, Sylvia, an American woman with a remarkable testimony of freedom from addiction, Maggie Smith from the church in Portsmouth, and a recent graduate, Chris Slater, to join the team with me.

In the summer of that year, we organised a series of children's Holiday Club outreaches in St Denys, Shirley, Eastleigh and Lordswood, which were attended by hundreds of children.

We had already supported the work of doctors Phil Clarke and Barry Trewinnard as they served the people on two large housing estates on the east side of the city. But Roger's encouragement to pursue a holistic approach to our mission added fuel to the fire. So, with much encouragement from the ebullient Colin Henderson, several caring initiatives were formed including Groundswell, a group focused on caring for those with HIV and AIDS as well as supporting their families, and Crossroads, a telephone listening service similar to the Samaritans.

We were doing what we could to proclaim the Good News creatively. We were actively seeking to care for those in need in our communities. So, in the autumn of 1984, Tony, Arthur and Martyn hosted an event in a virtually abandoned building in the centre of the city, Central Hall, looking at the supernatural dimension of our mission. This event was a conference focused of spiritual warfare, and was entitled Bind the Strong Man.

It felt significant for the event to be hosted at Central Hall. This was an old Methodist building that had been sold to the local authority in 1966, having been opened in 1925 as part of the Methodist Church's mission to the people working in and around the inner-city dock areas. It was now rarely used. We had received a prophetic word some years before that we 'would inherit a building our forefathers had laboured for'. Despite being cold and somewhat dingy, seeds of possibility were sown that would come to fruition in a few years' time.

John Wimber

Another event that had massive repercussions not just for our church, but for the Church across the nation in our pursuit of the supernatural dimension to our mission, was the visit of John Wimber to host a conference at the Methodist Westminster Central Hall in London.

David Watson, vicar at York's St Michael le Belfrey Anglican church, had met John Wimber while teaching together at the Fuller Theological Seminary in Pasadena, California. He had invited John to visit the UK and between 1981 and 1983, John had travelled to the UK several times, developing relationships with David in York, David Pytches at St Andrew's, Chorleywood, John Collins at Holy Trinity Brompton (HTB) and Baptist leader Douglas McBain.

Douglas McBain had organised the conference in London and opened the invitation to others beyond the small group of Anglicans and Baptists that had previously met John.

We had no idea who John Wimber was and as it happened, our newly formed evangelistic team had been invited to lead a mission at a teacher training college in Exeter when the conference at Westminster Central Hall had been organised. Dave Adcock was leading the mission with a Christian musician, Ray Bevan. Tony Rozee had been invited to the Wimber conference and asked if he could be excused from the Exeter outreach and attend the London event. Dave was happy for Tony to attend and so on Monday, 22nd October, the team headed down to Exeter and a couple of days later Tony made his way up to London for the John Wimber conference.

We had a reasonably good time at the teacher training college in Exeter. Dave spoke well each evening. Ray Bevan was very entertaining and a lot of fun to be with. We had many good conversations with students and headed home happy with our team's first major outreach.

I arrived home late morning on Saturday 27th, caught up with Caroline and then phoned Tony to see how he had got on at the John Wimber conference. He was so enthusiastic about what he had witnessed, he could hardly contain himself! He relayed stories of healing and deliverance. He had witnessed manifestations of Holy Spirit power that he had never seen before. He had experienced incredible encounters with God in worship. He had felt emboldened in his witness and was sharing Jesus with everyone he met.

As he shared, I felt so overwhelmed by the presence of God I literally fell over. My wife, Caroline, was really concerned for me. She had never seen me like this before. I said to her, 'We must go to London to see for ourselves.' Tony had told me that this would be the last night of the conference, and it was open to the public. I called Mike Pearson and asked if he wanted to come too. He did. And so Caroline, Mike and I set off for central London straight away.

We arrived about 5.00 p.m. By this time there was a queue of hundreds of people snaking its way around Central Hall. Small groups were worshipping and praying. I had heard stories of revival before. Was this it?

The doors opened at 6.00 p.m. and everyone flooded in. The place was full by 6.20 p.m. and the doors had to be closed. Another building was used as an overflow. Worship began early. The sense of reverence and awe was palpable. There were lots of new songs with a strong emphasis on intimacy, singing songs to Jesus rather than simply about him.

John Wimber came to the stage and began to speak. He spoke from Matthew 21:1-3:

> As they approached Jerusalem and came to Bethphage on the Mount of Olives, Jesus sent two disciples, saying to them, 'Go to the village ahead of you, and at once you

will find a donkey tied there, with her colt by her. Untie them and bring them to me. If anyone says anything to you, say that the Lord needs them, and he will send them right away.'

His message was simple, 'Jesus wants his Church back'!

He then called up some people who needed healing and prayed for them. As he prayed, he talked us through his method of praying, demystifying the process, to emphasise that this was something everyone could do. Or in his words, 'Everyone gets to play.'

Those who were prayed for testified to the healing and then he invited the Holy Spirit to come. There was an uncomfortable silence for a minute or two punctuated only by a cough here and there.

And then it happened.

All heaven broke loose.

As we looked around the auditorium there were people falling under the power of the Spirit, people whose arms were rotating helicopter-like, others shaking violently, others who were weeping, others laughing hysterically. The team with John Wimber were released to begin to minister to the crowd. Scores of men and women began to wander along the aisles laying hands on those 'manifesting', comforting those in distress and encouraging the work of the Holy Spirit.

Although I had felt a very dramatic personal encounter with the Holy Spirit, this was the first time I had experienced this level of encounter in a corporate setting. In our church settings we experienced a deep sense of presence in our worship and during the prayer ministry, but we had not seen this level of physical manifestation up to this point.

It's interesting to note that the Fountain Trust, the vehicle set up by Michael Harper and others in 1964 to foster renewal within the mainstream churches, had closed in 1980. And it was the visits of John Wimber from 1981 onwards that played a massive role in the acceleration of charismatic renewal within the mainstream denominations. The New Wine festivals and network, Soul Survivor, the HTB network and the Vineyard churches in the United Kingdom can all trace their roots back to these visits.

For us, in Southampton, this event was a catalyst that gave us fresh confidence to embrace and pursue the call to proclaim the gospel with 'words, works and wonders'.

Chapter Seven

GAINS AND LOSSES

In the spring of 1985, the church reached a significant milestone.

Ten years

Amazingly, we had arrived at our tenth anniversary. Over the May bank holiday weekend, members of the church congregation gathered at the picturesque Royal Victoria Country Park. The setting was idyllic, with sprawling green fields and the serene backdrop of the sea, creating a perfect atmosphere for an open-air celebration.

The festivities commenced with a variety of children's games for the youngest members of the congregation. There were sack races, egg-and-spoon races, and a treasure hunt that led the children through the park. Sports events followed, with both competitive and fun activities for all ages. By mid-afternoon the air was filled with the aroma of grilled food as the barbecue was set up. Long queues formed to purchase ice cream from the ice cream van that had arrived on site. The day concluded with a lively barn dance, the cheerful tunes of folk music echoing through the park, adding to the sense of joy and community.

The celebrations continued the next day on the evening of Tuesday, 28th May, with a special gathering at Southampton Guildhall. This historic venue, with its grand architecture and resonant acoustics, provided a fitting stage for an evening of reflection and gratitude. Just under 1,000 friends and members of the church filled the hall. The evening was filled with heartfelt worship and moving testimonies, where many expressed their profound gratitude to God for his blessings over the past decade. The atmosphere was charged with a sense of hope for the future as Tony set out the vision for the next ten years and beyond.

Increasing influence

By this milestone year, the church's influence had expanded significantly. What had started as a small and disparate gathering in the Centre for the Blind now had groups meeting on Sundays in eight different locations across the city – Woolston, Townhill Park, Highfield, Shirley, Freemantle, West End, Hollybrook and Lordswood. Each group brought its unique flavour and dynamic to the broader Church community, reflecting the diverse backgrounds and stories of its members. Additionally, nine new churches had been planted in the surrounding region, spreading the church's influence to Totton, Romsey, Eastleigh, Winchester, Andover, Hedge End, Gosport, Portsmouth and Havant.

Arthur Wallis, now a key member of the Cornerstone team and an elder of the church in Southampton, strongly influenced the way the church was being shaped as it grew. He had always carried a strong commitment to authentic expressions of Christian community. This commitment led to the strategy of favouring the formation of smaller local autonomous churches, rather than consolidating under a single large entity. His vision was clear: to empower communities to grow and thrive independently while maintaining a strong sense of unity and shared mission.

Regular all-church gatherings at the Boldrewood lecture theatre at the university provided a strong focal point for the groups that were meeting within the city. These meetings were more than just gatherings; they were vibrant expressions of shared faith and community. The hall had a capacity of around 400 and it was almost always full. The worship team had to get there early to set up and always led with great sensitivity and passion. This was the place for the leaders to articulate the vision and from time to time, guest speakers from across the globe would bring inspirational teaching. There was always opportunity for prayer ministry at the end and everyone would leave inspired and encouraged.

The regular celebration events hosted at Southampton Guildhall with visiting speakers, and the annual Bible Weeks that ran up until 1986, served as crucial connecting points for the other churches forming in the region.

The Cornerstone team extended their support beyond the local region, working with churches across the south-west of England, London, and internationally. Peter Light, known for his passionate faith and adventurous spirit, continued his visits to Asia. His journeys, often long and arduous, took him to remote areas where he worked tirelessly to spread the message of hope and love. In 1985 he travelled with Peter Howes, one of the leaders of the new church in Winchester, to Nepal, where the gospel had only arrived thirty years before. They connected with local leaders and church communities and shared their insights and faith.

Meanwhile, Geoff and Norah Wright embarked on a mission to Zambia. Their goal was to teach about Christian education, a subject close to their hearts. They travelled to different towns, bringing warmth and wisdom to the people they met. Martyn Dunsford and Phil Orchard visited Austria and Germany, sharing their experiences and strengthening ties with the churches there. Arthur and Eileen Wallis made connections with the church in mainland China during their time in Hong Kong, a city that has served as a bridge between cultures and continents. Tony Morton conducted ministry in Zimbabwe, making significant connections in the nation, while Dave Adcock spoke at a Bible Week in southern France, inspiring many with his words and insights.

The King's School was also growing from strength to strength. For four Sundays over the summer of 1984, the church cancelled its meetings and work parties took on the task of assisting with the construction of an extension at the West End site, adding a new gym hall, toilets and ancillary classrooms. By this stage there were around 100 children of primary school age and fifty of secondary school age.

The school continued to operate in the West End church building, and even with the expanded facilities it very quickly became necessary to look for alternative accommodation. Foulis Court, a large Victorian house in Fisher's Pond, on the edge of Southampton, was identified as an option. After much negotiation with the sellers and the local planning department, the church, in partnership with Eastleigh Christian Fellowship, purchased the property, and The King's School Senior was launched with David Trentham, who had recently moved from Bath, as headteacher, and Doug Williams, a teacher and member of the church in Chandler's Ford, taking responsibility to lead the primary school in West End.

Firgrove

Towards the end of 1984, Chris Thomas, the wife of Adrian, had challenged the church's leadership on their stance regarding abortion. This pivotal moment led Phil Clarke, along with his wife, Sheelagh, also a health professional, to attend a conference in Phoenix, Arizona. Hosted by Dave and Joanne Everitt, the conference focused on the development of crisis pregnancy centres. Inspired by this experience, Phil and Sheelagh returned with a vision to establish a similar centre in Southampton.

A steering group was formed, and the church rallied together to raise £13,000 to launch the Firgrove Centre, located close to King's House in Firgrove Road. The centre quickly became a vital resource, offering support and care to women in need. Over the next few years, it supported thousands of women and inspired the development of around 160 other centres across the UK.

Spreading the Word

In the summer of 1985, the church hosted its third Bible Week at Shepton Mallet, attracting around 3,000 attendees. The events were a massive undertaking, requiring meticulous planning and coordination led ably by Colin Henderson. Members from Southampton Community Church provided essential administrative support and ministry throughout the week. The church's musicians led the worship team. The children's team managed the J-team programme for kids under twelve, offering engaging and fun-filled activities that helped the children connect with their faith. Volunteers from the congregation handled catering, hospitality and site maintenance, fostering a sense of community and shared purpose.

That summer of 1985 also marked a significant mobilisation of evangelism. Organised by the Cornerstone evangelism team, the Five Days for God campaign invited individuals to engage in five days of outreach across fifteen locations in the south of England, as well as in Zürich and the island of Jersey. Nearly 200 people participated, resulting in successful outreaches in Barnstaple, Minehead, Bridgwater, Salisbury, Winchester, Kingston, Hampton, Portchester, Lee-on-the-Solent, Southsea, Isle of Wight, Jersey and Zürich. Each location brought its unique challenges and opportunities, but the unified effort and shared mission led to profound impacts and lasting connections.

Reaching out

We began working with disaffected young people on the streets of our city, aiming to provide support, guidance and hope to those in need. This initiative marked a significant step in our commitment to reaching out to marginalised groups and making a tangible difference in their lives.

In addition to our local efforts, we hosted an International Leaders' Event that brought together around thirty of our overseas connections from Nepal, India, Belgium, France and Zimbabwe. This event fostered a sense of global unity and collaboration, highlighting the importance of building strong, supportive relationships with our international partners. It was a time of sharing experiences, learning from each other, and strengthening our collective mission.

In August 1986, we held the fourth and final Bible Week at Shepton Mallet, which became famously known as The South and *Wet* Bible Week due to the challenging weather conditions. Despite the rain, it was the most successful Bible Week yet, drawing large crowds and leaving a lasting impact on all who attended. That year I was responsible for the work among our children, and the theme of Billy and the Bungle Jungle Gang created a memorable experience. Many young people recall this week as a pivotal moment in their spiritual journeys, where they gave their lives to Christ and were filled with the Holy Spirit.

By the summer of 1986, our evangelistic efforts extended beyond our local community as we mobilised teams to spread the message of the gospel in Germany, Switzerland, France,

London, Devon and Somerset. These missions reflected our broader vision and commitment to sharing God's love and message with people far and wide.

During this period, we were not simply operating as a local church with a traditional focus on the congregation or 'parish'. Instead, we were evolving into an apostolic community. A local church typically has a clearly defined area of mission, often indicated by its name, such as Millbrook Baptist Church or Bitterne Methodist Church, which suggests a focus on a specific geographic area or housing estate.

However, our calling was to be something different. We were called to be an apostolic community, with Tony, our main leader at the time, graced by God to serve as an apostle. There was some nervousness around the use of the term apostle or apostolic, but at its core, the word 'apostle' simply means 'the one who is sent'. Thus, the hallmark of an apostle and an apostolic community is their unwavering commitment to God's mission. While all churches have some apostolic elements, our unique calling was to be apostolic to the city, the nation and the nations. This was evident in the breadth and depth of our missional engagement during these first ten years.

The focus on being an apostolic community was not just a passing phase but a foundational theme that would continue to shape our identity and actions in the years ahead. Our journey up to 1986 laid the groundwork for a future where our commitment to God's mission would remain at the forefront of all we did, continually driving us to reach out, support and transform lives across the globe.

A pivotal point

Up to this point, we had found things relatively easy. Most of the things that we tried worked. There had been one or two leadership challenges but nothing major. We had faced some opposition from other church leaders in the city, who accused us of 'sheep stealing' or worse, leading people into error. However, there had been no division or scandal. And as the original leaders were moving to wider ministries, new leaders were stepping up. Allan Cox and Phil Orchard had recently joined the staff team, bringing fresh perspectives and renewed energy.

But these years in the mid-1980s did bring us some unexpected challenges.

We experienced loss for the first time.

Dave and Carolyn Adcock faced an unimaginable tragedy when they lost their twin boys, who were born prematurely, in April of 1985. Another family lost a child over that summer. These devastating events cast a shadow over the church, bringing the first real encounter with death to a mostly young congregation. The shock and grief rippled through the community, bringing a sobering reminder of life's fragility.

Over the next twelve months, this heartbreak was to become a regular and harrowing feature.

A member of the church who worked as a builder tragically fell from scaffolding and died, leaving behind a grieving family. In another heartbreaking incident, one of the much-loved group leaders from the West End gathering was killed in a sudden and tragic car crash. Arthur and Eileen Wallis' fourteen-year-old granddaughter, Katrina, also died tragically from peritonitis. The string of sorrow continued as several babies succumbed to the unexplained cot death phenomenon. First one, then two, then a third and a fourth, all within a matter of months, leaving the community in a state of profound grief and confusion.

By this time, the church elders were deeply concerned that this series of deaths was not merely coincidental but might indicate something more sinister at work. Could this be the work of the enemy, seeking to discourage us and instil fear in our hearts just as we were witnessing God's work in our midst? Could our new focus on addressing the issue of abortion be a contributing factor?

Faced with these questions and their own grief, the elders called the church to a time of fasting and prayer. They organised a special prayer meeting at King's House, inviting everyone to come together to stand against what they perceived as a pattern of death. The atmosphere was thick with emotion as we cried out to God, taking authority over the work of the enemy with fervent prayer and worship.

I attended the meeting, but my wife, Caroline, stayed at home with our newly born son, David. I must admit, we were fearful that maybe he was next. My prayers were heartfelt and intense, driven by a deep concern for our baby boy. Caroline prayed at home with David in his Moses basket next to her. As we prayed at King's House and Caroline prayed at home, she was led to a comforting scripture in the Psalms. Psalm 91:16 says, 'With long life I will satisfy him and show him my salvation.'

This verse brought her a sense of peace, affirming that God had heard our prayers and that our son would not die. After a couple of hours of intense prayer and worship at King's House, we all felt a similar sense of breakthrough.

Although we felt confident that we had made a breakthrough, it wasn't until a few months later that we were fully assured. A visiting American preacher, Terry Law, spoke at a church gathering at the Boldrewood lecture theatre.

He began by sharing a dream he had while preparing to visit us. In the dream, he saw a dark cloud that was seeking to overwhelm us as a church. He had no prior knowledge of what we had been experiencing. He shared that in the dream, God's light rose and dispelled the cloud. He declared, 'Whatever has been coming against you, today the cloud has been dispelled.'

As you can imagine, we were profoundly encouraged that the Lord had seen our tears and heard our prayers.

Spiritual warfare

This was probably the first time we sensed the reality of the spiritual battle that we were engaged with. We had embarked on this journey with youthful enthusiasm and excitement, and here we were, ten years on, being confronted with the fact that our battle wasn't against 'flesh and blood, but against the rulers, against the authorities, against the powers of this dark world and against the spiritual forces of evil in the heavenly realms' (Ephesians 6:12).

We didn't change our theology or practice and bring undue emphasis on 'spiritual warfare' as some of our contemporaries had done. Our position was, and remains, that God is greater than anything that the enemy would seek to throw at us. We took great comfort from the psalmist when he states that God prepares a table for us in the presence of our enemies (Psalm 23:5), and he invites us to that table to experience his presence in the midst of challenge, difficulty and pain. We don't need to shout and holler or stamp our feet but simply rest in him, be secure in our identity in Christ and speak with the authority that he has given us.

During this season, one of the members of the worship team, Dave Evans, penned the words of what has become one of the most popular new hymns in the UK. The song encapsulates what we were experiencing and learning at that time.

> Be still, for the presence of the Lord,
> the holy One, is here;
> come bow before him now
> with reverence and fear
> in him no sin is found
> we stand on holy ground.
> Be still, for the presence of the Lord,
> the holy One, is here.
>
> Be still, for the glory of the Lord
> is shining all around;
> he burns with holy fire,
> with splendour he is crowned:
> how awesome is the sight

our radiant king of light!
Be still, for the glory of the Lord
is shining all around.

Be still, for the power of the Lord
is moving in this place:
he comes to cleanse and heal,
to minister his grace –
no work too hard for him.
In faith receive from him.
Be still, for the power of the Lord
is moving in this place.

This season brought a sense of sobriety to us as a church community but didn't cause us to retreat or withdraw from the mission we sensed God had called us to.

Chapter Eight

WHAT ABOUT THE WOMEN?

There are a couple of significant things that you would immediately notice if you attended one of our meetings in the 1970s and 1980s.

The first was that the leaders, called elders, would always be seated at the front of the meeting hall or venue. Not on the front row facing the platform but on the platform itself, alongside the musicians and the worship leader, facing the congregation. What you would also notice about these elders was that they were all men.

The second noticeable thing was that all the women in the congregation would be wearing a headscarf. This wasn't simply a fashion statement, as the scarf would be removed as soon as the meeting ended, but was an explicit teaching in the church at the time that referenced the role of men and women in the church.

Some key elements of the teaching that shaped early Restoration theology and practice to do with gender roles were the nature of spiritual authority and the importance of restoring God's order in the Church and the family.

The teaching was, in some ways, a reaction to changing attitudes in society at large during the 1960s. This period was marked by significant social, cultural and political change, with shifts in attitudes and values impacting various aspects of society. The decade saw a movement towards a more permissive society where traditional moral constraints on sexual behaviour were questioned and often rejected. This led to debates about the moral implications of these changes, including concerns about the erosion of family values and the potential consequences for societal stability.

Influence of the feminist movement

Alongside these societal changes, the feminist movement of the 1960s, which sought gender equality and women's rights, presented challenges and opportunities for the Church. Some Christian denominations began to re-examine and challenge traditional gender roles and support women's ordination and leadership. Others, including those influential in the Restoration movement, resisted these changes, upholding traditional views on gender and family roles.

Arthur Wallis articulated these concerns in an article titled 'Women in the Plan of God' in the July 1979 edition of *Restoration Magazine*. He stated:

The family is the cornerstone of the nation. The breakdown of family life spells the disintegration of society. That this is happening before our very eyes with one marriage in three ending in the divorce courts is all too evident. We need to realise that this is the result of a satanic strategy. Indiscriminate sex, free love, adultery, and homosexuality are now viewed as unavoidable, if not socially acceptable. This has put our civilisation in the greatest peril. It is Satan's gigantic con-trick all in the name of progress and liberalisation to destroy God's order for the family. Never was there such an opportunity for the Christian community to demonstrate the beauty, harmony, and blessedness of God's alternative society.

The motivation was clear: the creation of an alternative society where God's order and ways were followed to the letter. Arthur acknowledged that women had important contributions to make but was adamant that leadership was not one of them. He wrote:

While recognising the many valuable, indeed, indispensable roles that God has given to a woman in the work of his Kingdom, it appears that the leading of men and ruling over men are not among them. It is not a question of whether they have the ability but whether God has invested them with the authority.

Thus, in our church, as in most churches in the Restoration movement at that time, leadership was very clearly male and, therefore, only men could be appointed as elders.

The Plymouth Brethren

It is also worth noting that quite a few of the influential leaders within the emerging Restoration movement had roots in the Plymouth Brethren. The attitudes towards women in leadership and gender roles within the Plymouth Brethren during the 1960s and 1970s were characterised by strict adherence to traditional, conservative Christian beliefs. They believed firmly in male leadership both in the church and in the household.

Within the Plymouth Brethren, women were not allowed to take on leadership roles in the church. Elders, pastors and any form of church leadership were roles exclusively reserved for men. Women were expected to remain silent during church services, in accordance with 1 Corinthians 14:34-35. Women's participation was largely limited to non-leadership roles, such as organising social events, teaching children and other supportive activities.

Traditional gender roles were also promoted within the family structure. Men were seen as the primary breadwinners and spiritual heads of the household, while women were encouraged to focus on homemaking, child-rearing and supporting their husbands.

Education for women was often limited, as higher education and professional careers were not typically encouraged for women within the Plymouth Brethren community. Instead, the focus was on preparing women for their roles as wives and mothers.

These attitudes were reflective of a broader conservative evangelical Christian ethos during that period, but were particularly stringent within the Plymouth Brethren due to their literal interpretation of the Bible and emphasis on maintaining distinct boundaries from mainstream society.

It was this line of thinking that shaped the theology and practice of the emerging house churches in the 1970s and 1980s.

Authority and submission

Another strong emphasis that came through in the early years of the Restoration movement was the topic of authority and submission.

Ern Baxter famously delivered a series of talks at the Lakes Bible Week in 1975 entitled, 'The Head and Shoulders Man', where he compared the leadership of King Saul, called to be king because he was 'head and shoulders' (1 Samuel 9:2, NLT) above everyone else, versus King David, who was anointed by Samuel to be king despite the fact he had no notable physical features that made him stand out. Baxter likened this to many of the leaders in current mainstream churches who may be 'head and shoulders' above others in terms of academic achievement, or public speaking ability, or organisational management, but lack the clear anointing of the Holy Spirit for leadership of the Church of Jesus Christ.

In his teaching he made it clear that all authority had been given to Christ, from the Father, and this authority was delegated to men, chosen by God to lead his Church.

In many cases at this time, churches were governed by committee or the church meeting rather than having leaders, chosen and anointed by God, who were given the right to lead as they felt led by God.

Hence, if God had anointed a leader, it was up to those in the congregation to submit to that leader and follow his direction. This was part of what was meant by restoring order to the Church.

This delegated authority or 'headship' as referred to in 1 Corinthians 11, crossed over from the church to the home. It was taught that the husband is the head of his wife, as Christ is the head of man, and in the same way that men are to submit to Christ, their head, wives were called to submit to their husbands. This was seen as God's order for marriage and the family.

It was in this same passage in 1 Corinthians 11 where head coverings were mentioned:

> But every woman who prays or prophesies with her head uncovered dishonours her head – it is the same as having her head shaved. For if a woman does not cover her head, she might as well have her hair cut off; but if it is a disgrace for a woman to have her hair cut off or her head shaved, then she should cover her head.
>
> A man ought not to cover his head, since he is the image and glory of God; but woman is the glory of man. For man did not come from woman, but woman from man; neither was man created for woman, but woman for

man. It is for this reason that a woman ought to have authority over her own head, because of the angels.

(vv. 5-10)

This was the common teaching in Plymouth Brethren circles long before the Restoration movement emerged. And in the new movement's desire to fully embrace New Testament Church practice, the wearing of headscarves by women in meetings became commonplace.

Critics have since argued that the Restoration movement often exhibited a top-down, authoritarian leadership style, where church leaders wielded significant control over congregants' lives. This led to accusations of spiritual abuse and manipulation. The leaders were sometimes seen as being above reproach, with little or no mechanisms in place for accountability. This unchecked power was seen as a fertile ground for abuses.

The emphasis on submission to Church authority was criticised for suppressing individual thought and discouraging alternative interpretations of the Scriptures. Members were often expected to conform strictly to the leaders' teachings. And the movement's strict adherence to traditional gender roles was seen as perpetuating patriarchal structures, marginalising women, and limiting their opportunities for leadership and personal development.

These criticisms highlighted the tension between the movement's desire to return to what it perceived as the original, pure form of Christianity and the broader societal shifts towards individualism, gender equality and democratic forms of governance.

Many of those who were now members of the church had little previous church background or, if they did, they were from the more traditional Church of England, Roman Catholic or Baptist traditions.

Many, including most of the women, had come from more middle-class backgrounds and had been university trained, and although they initially accepted the teaching and practices around gender roles, authority and submission, over time they began to question the validity of such practices.

Consequently, over the years, several decisions were made that shifted the church towards a more egalitarian position.

Decisions

Sometime around 1986, Arthur Wallis delivered a talk to the church at one of the all-church midweek meetings at the Boldrewood lecture theatre at the university. He spoke from the 1 Corinthians 11 passage on headship and head coverings. The eldership team had been discussing this issue recently and had come to some conclusions.

The reason that women were commanded to have their heads covered, according to Arthur's interpretation of the Scripture, was 'as a sign of authority' and 'because of the angels'. Therefore, he asserted, the purpose for the wearing of a head covering should be to increase a women's sense of confidence in their authority. However, the elders recognised the opposite was now true and women in the church were feeling less confident and often feeling inferior to the men in the room.

Arthur also pointed out that the scripture did not say that women should have their heads covered when they gathered for worship but only when they prayed or prophesied, which the elders took to mean, praying or prophesying publicly. Therefore, the decision was made that women would no longer need to have their heads covered when we met for worship, and it was up to the individual woman whether they chose to wear a head covering when they prayed or prophesied publicly.

The answer was emphatic. At the next public meeting there was only one woman wearing a headscarf.

It was a small step. But a significant one.

Up to this point when an elder was appointed, although the husband was the one being appointed to the role, the wife would also be recognised alongside him. So, it was John *and* Jenny, Allan *and* Lizzie and Phil *and* Maggie who were recognised and prayed for. Because of the expectation that a wife's main function was to support her husband, the wife didn't really have a lot of choice but to accept the position and role that was being given to her husband. Some wives flourished in this supportive role and enjoyed the contribution that they were able to make to the life and ministry of the church. Others didn't feel that they had any contribution to make but felt guilty that they didn't feel the same way as others.

Tony and the other elders recognised this and made the decision that wives of elders no longer needed to feel obligated to serve alongside their husbands but should be released to pursue their own sense of individual calling. This was another significant step that released many of these women to follow the careers that they had trained for without feeling guilty, and without the obligation to attend regular eldership meetings or other leadership functions.

By the early 1990s the elders, or leaders, were no longer sitting on the platform, or at the front of the meeting venue. Leadership was to be seen as a grace gift, given by Christ, to serve the body and not as a function that placed individuals 'over' the congregation but recognised them within the community from where they exercised that leadership.

By the mid-1990s the decision was made to drop the term 'elder'. Tony argued that it was hard to get around the fact that the Greek word for 'elder' was male and, therefore, if the leadership of the church was governed by 'elders' then that would inevitably be a body of men. Tony therefore made the decision that we would no longer use the term 'elder' to describe those who carried leadership responsibility in the church, but we would simply use the term 'leader'.

From the early days of the church, right back to the Agape Fellowship, women along with men had been functioning with leadership responsibility, not just supportive roles. Women had been leading worship, working pastorally, preaching, teaching, prophesying, involved in decision-making and carrying spiritual responsibility.

And so, over these formative years the understanding of leadership, gender roles, authority and submission was reformed, and a leadership team emerged that better reflected the convictions held. A team that involved men and women, married and single, who would take responsibility for the oversight and future direction of the church.

These small incremental changes proved to be the beginning of much greater gender equality within the church, recognising the contributions of both men and women in leadership roles and allowing for a more inclusive and supportive church environment.

Chapter Nine

GROWTH AND INFLUENCE

It's now 1987, and despite the assertion by Andrew Walker, in *Restoring the Kingdom*,[3] that growth in the Restoration movement peaked around 1985, we were continuing to grow and develop. What we were finding was that the movement of Christians from one church to another was no longer an active factor in our growth. We had committed ourselves to innovate in our mission and make the most of the opportunities that were opening up for us.

March for Jesus

To publicly express our faith and unity, the church joined with hundreds of other cities in organising a March for Jesus event in the city centre. This occasion attracted more than 800 participants, demonstrating significant local support and enthusiasm.

During the summer of 1987, the church partnered with British Youth for Christ to host an evangelism programme called

Street Invaders. This initiative brought together forty young people for two weeks of outreach activities. The theme song for the outreach became 'Shine, Jesus, Shine', one of the main songs written by Graham Kendrick for March for Jesus. The song reflected the mission to spread the light and love of Christ to the people of Southampton. Activities included street performances, handing out literature and engaging in conversations about faith, as well as several evening outreach events.

Events and conferences

Instead of organising a weeklong Bible Week in the summer, the Cornerstone team planned weekend Breakout events in different locations: Selsey, Weymouth and the island of Jersey. These events were designed to provide concentrated times of worship, teaching and fellowship, enabling participants to be inspired in their faith and deepen connections.

The church hosted an evangelism conference and a worship conference at The King's School venue over separate weekends in the autumn. These conferences featured guest speakers, workshops and seminars focused on equipping attendees with skills and inspiration for both evangelism and worship.

Leaders from the church were again active in international missions, with Martyn Dunsford visiting Germany, Austria and Switzerland; Peter Light and David Damp travelling to Nepal; Ken Ford accompanying Peter Light to Thailand and Malaysia; and Dave Adcock making multiple trips to France.

Additionally, Tony went to minister in Spain with Peter Stott, leader of the church in Havant.

In a strategic move, the church leadership decided to consolidate the Sunday gatherings into three larger area meetings: one meeting at Itchen College in Bitterne, another in Portswood near the university, and a third in Shirley. These gatherings were again supplemented by monthly all-church meetings held at the Boldrewood lecture theatre, that fostered a sense of unity and shared vision among the wider Church body.

Further initiatives

We also initiated a series of outreach events called Encounters at a local hotel. These evenings featured music, testimony, drama and a gospel message, offering attendees an opportunity to respond to the Christian faith. These events aimed to create an inviting and non-threatening atmosphere for non-churchgoers to explore Christianity.

We produced a newspaper, *Ordinary People*, which was printed at the *Daily Echo* print workshop. This publication contained personal testimonies and articles designed to convey the message of the gospel in a relatable and accessible manner.

In early 1988, the church invited Reinhard Bonnke, a renowned German evangelist and founder of Christ for all Nations (CfaN), to hold a series of outreach meetings at Southampton Guildhall. Bonnke was famous for his large-scale evangelistic meetings, particularly in Africa, where his events drew millions and were marked by reports of thousands of healings and conversions.

His visit to Southampton attracted many hundreds of people from across the region, with reports of healings and people coming to faith, reflecting the powerful impact of his ministry.

However, we did also hit a few 'bumps in the road' in these years.

Managing the bumps

The King's School had grown in numbers and influence since its launch in 1982. The school was classed as a private independent school funded by the fees paid by parents and underwritten by the church. The school was not independent financially but sat within the legal framework of Southampton Community Church. We took advice when we were setting up the school and the decision was made that parents would simply donate to the church, the church could then claim Gift Aid, equivalent to an additional 20 per cent, and the funds would be forwarded to the school to pay for teaching staff and resources.

After five years of this arrangement, Her Majesty's Revenue and Customs (HMRC) reviewed the way that we had set up the financial processes and concluded that this was not an acceptable way to fund the school, as those who were donating, that is the parents, were benefiting from their donations in the form of their children's education.

The result was that the church was issued with a large five-figure sum tax bill that needed to be paid. We negotiated a payment plan with HMRC but it did mean we had to make significant cuts to our expenditure and the decision was made to reduce staffing costs to alleviate the burden.

Rather than make roles redundant, it was decided to reduce the working hours of some members of staff. Dave Adcock and Phil Orchard were both qualified teachers and were asked to return to teaching part-time for a period. I was offered a revised job role, as head of youth, and given a monthly retainer, but was encouraged to get a full-time job. Because of my background in retail management, I was able to secure a management role at the local John Lewis department store, Tyrell & Green, quite quickly.

Other roles were merged and new responsibilities allocated. Tony Rozee became head of evangelism and formed the Here & Now team with Denis Birch and Phil Rowlands, two recognised evangelists who were members of the wider Cornerstone family of churches. Allan Cox broadened his pastoral responsibilities to cover the gaps left by Phil Orchard and Dave Adcock's change of roles.

Another shock to the system was the decision that Martyn Dunsford would relocate to Hedge End, stepping away from his responsibilities for the church in Southampton. Martyn was now a key leader within the church and the wider Cornerstone network and worked very closely with Tony, Arthur and the other leaders. He had taken responsibility for the oversight of the church on the north and east sides of the city from Highfield in the north, across to Bitterne Park on the east of the River Itchen and down to Woolston at the south end of the east side.

Tony had suggested to Martyn that he should consider relocating to pursue his calling. He suggested a number of possible options for Martyn. Martyn and his wife, Gaynor, took some time out to pray and discern God's will for them as a family and settled on the idea of moving to Hedge End to take responsibility for the church there as well as oversee the churches that had been planted on the edge of the city, including Eastleigh, Chandler's Ford and Bishop's Waltham. In addition, Martyn would remain a member of the Cornerstone team and continue his work into Germany, Austria and Switzerland.

This wasn't an uncommon occurrence in Restoration circles at that time. There are numerous stories of people being moved from church to church and place to place without much process or consultation. It was the prevailing culture. In these first few years, Caroline and I were asked to consider moving to several different locations. First Uxbridge to plant a new church, then East Acton to take on the leadership of an already existing church, and then, sometime later, Dorchester, where an opportunity to start a new church had come up. We didn't feel that any of those options fitted with what we sensed God had called us to, so we stayed where we were.

The dilemma for us had been the fact that Martyn and Gaynor had been acting as our pastors as we embarked on married life and had begun our roles in leadership. We didn't really know Tony and Hannah very well. Martyn did ask if we wanted to move with them to the new church in Hedge End, but we didn't feel that was the right thing for us either.

We arranged to meet with Tony and Hannah and were reassured that we could see a way where we could be supported and grow under their leadership. Tony made it clear that he had made the decision with Martyn's best interests at heart and this opportunity would enable Martyn to grow into all that God had called him to. Today, the 1,000-strong King's Community Church in Hedge End is testament to Martyn's leadership and calling.

I started work at Tyrell & Green in April 1988. Because of work we were unable to attend any of the Breakout events that had been organised, or the summer outreach weeks that the Here & Now team were facilitating. We were focused on developing the youth work across the church with the growing number of teenagers, as well as outreach to the various groups that we had connected with over the past few summers. It didn't leave us with a lot of time for much else.

However, the biggest shock to the system was still to come.

Spiritual father

One day, in August of 1988, Tony and Hannah came into the store where I was working. They had concern etched over their faces. They had some sad news to share with me. Arthur Wallis, the de facto spiritual father of the church, had died the day before. He had been on retreat with Bryn Jones' apostolic team at a conference centre near Sheffield. He was only sixty-five.

Arthur's son, Jonathan, relayed the story of Arthur's last moments before his death in his book *Arthur Wallis: Radical Christian*:

In the afternoon of the first day of the retreat, Arthur shared some things that God had been saying to him from the book of Ephesians about the centrality of Christ in all that they were believing for. Throughout the day the earnestness in prayer and seeking God was matched by a sense of enjoyment as they relaxed together, completely at home in the Father's presence.

It was a warm August evening and after their meal, they sat outside drinking coffee and chatting together. Arthur was talking with Keri Jones when someone suggested a game of croquet before it got too dark. Keri had never played the game before but as an ex-physical education teacher he decided to give it a go.

'Come on my young brother,' Arthur said, 'I'll teach you.' They played in pairs, and Arthur partnered Ivor Hopkins. As Keri found his ball frequently and ruthlessly dispatched to the other end of the lawn, he began to wonder whether Arthur was giving him an object lesson in humility rather than teaching him to play the game. It soon became apparent who was going to win.

'Well done, Arthur, you've won,' exclaimed Keri, as Arthur hit the final peg with his ball. 'Three cheers for Arthur!'

Arthur smiled with the satisfaction of a born competitor 'I haven't finished yet,' he replied, 'I must go and help my partner.'

He strode purposely back across the lawn towards Ivor. As he approached the wooden cross, he faltered and suddenly fell face forward onto the grass. The others ran to his aid but all efforts to revive him were of no avail. He had died instantly of a massive heart attack.

Keri couldn't help wondering whether the first words he heard in heaven corresponded with the last words he heard on earth: 'Well done, Arthur, you've won.'[4]

This would be a huge loss for the church, for the wider Restoration movement across the UK, and even further afield.

Arthur had been a prominent figure in the charismatic renewal and Restoration movements from the early 1950s. He had been a key influence in the development of the church, and his relocation to Southampton had been a blessing to all of us.

Arthur's presence and demeanour were both a source of comfort and inspiration. His gentle nature made him approachable, and his impeccable appearance reflected his disciplined life. His sense of humour often lightened the atmosphere, making it easier for everyone to connect and engage in meaningful discussions.

It was only in the last couple of years that I got to know Arthur and his wife, Eileen. Caroline and I had been invited to be part of a small leadership development group that met weekly at their home, along with six other couples. This setting provided a great opportunity for us to get to know Arthur and Eileen very well.

I also remember with some trepidation delivering my first talk to one of the area setting gatherings. I was nervous enough, but the sight of Arthur Wallis sitting in front of me was somewhat intimidating. I did manage to get through the talk without too much difficulty but was acutely aware that I needed to make sure that what I was saying was theologically accurate.

Arthur was not only a mentor but also a friend to so many. His insights into spiritual matters and his commitment to the principles of Restoration theology and practice were evident in every interaction. Through his leadership and personal example, Arthur significantly shaped the lives of those around him, encouraging them to pursue a deeper relationship with God and to embrace the transformative power of the Holy Spirit.

Arthur's legacy continued to influence and inspire many within the Restoration and charismatic renewal movements. His dedication, humility and gentle spirit were remembered fondly by all who had the privilege of knowing him. The church in Southampton, where Arthur was based, particularly missed him following his death in 1988. His absence left a profound void in the community he so faithfully served. Arthur's impact on the church was immense. His life reminded us of the importance of leadership that is rooted in humility and driven by a genuine desire to serve others.

Chapter Ten

Big Church

In the late 1980s, a subtle yet profound shift began to unfold within our church community, marking the start of a new era. Up until that point, our history had been characterised by the formation of small, intimate groups and house churches, which gradually grew and evolved into larger congregations meeting in school halls and community centres.

Our strategy was strongly influenced by Arthur Wallis, who had roots in the Plymouth Brethren, and a deep commitment to genuine and authentic community. We had therefore focused on the development of networks of smaller, autonomous churches across the city and region. This approach was also shaped by the fact that we did not own any large church buildings at the time, which naturally lent itself to a model of dispersed, smaller gatherings rather than the establishment of a single, large congregation.

New model

The transformation of this approach was notably articulated in the January 1987 edition of *Restoration Magazine*. In an interview, Terry Virgo, the leader of the Brighton-based Newfrontiers apostolic network, was asked about the future direction of his ministry. He responded with a vision that would come to influence many, saying:

> We were gathering for three days of fasting and prayer for the nation and for the media when God spoke to us prophetically: 'You're not ready for the nation. The way I'll speak to the nation is by raising up large churches. Then the media will come to you to ask what's happening.'

Virgo reflected on the experience of his own church, sharing that although the plan initially was to plant a separate church on the other side of Brighton, he felt a divine prompting to keep the congregations together and build something larger:

> In the Brighton and Hove area, when we subdivided our congregation eighteen months ago, I thought we would just plant a separate church on the other side of town. But I felt God tell me to hold the two groups together. Now we've divided into five congregations but we're keeping it as one church and believing God to build something large.

He cited the example of Paul's ministry in Ephesus from Acts 19, where a small group grew into a significant church that played a vital role in the spread of Christianity throughout Asia

Minor. Virgo's words marked a significant shift in thinking, from a focus on smaller, autonomous churches to the idea of building large, impactful congregations.

This new perspective resonated within the leadership team of Southampton Community Church as well. The team grappled with the question of whether it was time for change in church structure, whether the time had come to transition from multiple small gatherings to a unified, larger congregation.

Local response

In response to these reflections, a pivotal decision was made. It was agreed that at the end of 1988, the church would consolidate its various area settings in Bitterne, Highfield and Shirley, ceasing their separate meetings to come together as one unified congregation every Sunday morning at the Boldrewood lecture theatre, beginning in early 1989. This decision marked the start of a new chapter in the life of the church.

As these meetings gathered momentum, the idea of finding a permanent home for the church became a more regular topic of conversation. There had been a conviction in the church that God would give us a building that 'our forefathers had laboured for'. Over the preceding years, several church buildings in the area had been sold and repurposed as mosques and Sikh gurdwaras, which heightened the sense of opportunity and legacy surrounding the search for a new space.

While Boldrewood was a functional venue for the church's meetings, it had its limitations. The space was not always available every week, and there were very few breakout rooms for children's activities. Consequently, the decision was made to hire a property consultant to explore available land and buildings in Southampton. The consultant discovered that Central Hall, the former Methodist building located in the heart of the city, might soon be on the market. We had previously used Central Hall for an event in the early 1980s, and the idea of acquiring it seemed promising.

Initial informal discussions were held with Hampshire County Council, the then-owners of Central Hall, and a preliminary offer was tentatively accepted. However, when Southampton City Council, now a unitary authority separate from Hampshire County Council, became aware of the potential sale, they sought to intervene. Southampton City Council wanted to acquire the building for use as an arts venue and thus challenged the decision-making process. As a result, Hampshire County Council announced that the sale would be conducted by sealed bids that would need to be submitted by 16th May 1990, and the highest bid would determine the outcome.

In response, we decided to increase our original bid from £450,000 to £520,000, anticipating that Southampton City Council would make a competitive offer. On 17th May 1990, we received the exciting news from the Hampshire County Council officer that our bid had been successful. This news was met with immense joy and celebration within the church community; however, Southampton City Council were not so happy. They immediately went back to Hampshire County Council with a higher offer, but Hampshire refused to accept it as the process was clear and our sealed bid had been accepted.

The *Daily Echo*, Southampton's local newspaper, covered the story, highlighting Southampton City Council's disappointment over what they saw as the loss of a significant city asset. We endeavoured to reassure the public of our intentions to use the building to serve the community and contribute positively to the city's cultural and spiritual life.

Special Offering

Several weeks later, during one of our Sunday morning gatherings at the Boldrewood lecture theatre, we took up a special offering to support the purchase and refurbishment of Central Hall. The occasion was marked by joyous celebration, with flag waving, singing and dancing as the congregation pledged over £100,000 towards the project. Additionally, we arranged to sell our existing property, King's House in Shirley, and secured a loan from a bank to cover the remaining costs.

By the autumn of that year, the purchase was finalised and we were working towards holding our first meeting in Central Hall on the Sunday after Easter Sunday, 1991. It was a significant milestone, not only because of the acquisition itself but also because of the historical and spiritual significance of the building we had inherited.

Central Hall had originally been established as a centre for mission by the Methodists in February 1925. However, as the congregation dwindled in the mid-1960s, the building was sold to Hampshire County Council. Under the stewardship of the County Council, the building fell into a state of disrepair as it was repurposed as an annex of City College, with only the classrooms and small hall in use.

In the final edition of the Methodist's *Central Hall Magazine* in 1965, the editor, C.W. Block, penned a farewell message imbued with hope for the future:

> As my wife and I sever our connection with Central Hall, we pray that there may be many more chapters still to be written in which the Lord may be glorified, and men and women brought to the knowledge of His saving grace.

This message struck a chord with us, as we found ourselves in a position to fulfil Mr Block's prayer and continue the legacy of Central Hall's mission.

Original vision

We were also deeply moved to learn about the original vision behind the Methodist Central Halls, established across the country in the early twentieth century. The vision was initiated in 1891, marking the centenary of John Wesley's death, with the aim of creating a great memorial to Wesley's life and work. It was not until 1898 that the Wesleyan Methodist Conference launched the Wesleyan Methodist Twentieth Century Fund, known as the Million Guinea Fund, to finance this ambitious project. The goal was to raise £1 million from Methodists across the country, with contributions coming primarily from ordinary church members.

They were successful – the fund ultimately raised just over £1 million, equivalent to more than £57 million in today's money. Of this, a quarter was allocated to the construction of the Central Hall in Westminster, which opened in 1912. The remainder of the funds were used for new chapels, missions, education and other charitable causes.

More than 100 Central Halls were established during this period as part of the Methodist Church's Forward Movement, up to the late 1930s. They were designed not only as places of worship but also as community centres that addressed the spiritual, social and educational needs of their local populations.

In Southampton, the Methodist congregation in East Street had been operating a centre for mission to the surrounding dockland community. The local Methodist Circuit decided to launch a fundraising campaign to purchase land and build Southampton's Central Hall. As with the fundraising for Westminster Central Hall, ordinary people pledged money, but the project was greatly aided by the generosity of a wealthy businessman, Joseph Rank, father of J. Arthur Rank, the founder of the film and media company Rank Organisation, owners of Odeon cinemas and Pinewood Studios. The building was opened to the public on 18th February 1925. The total cost of the project was £41,000.

In the opening leaflet, the minister, Rev. Arthur Boyce, made the following statement:

> Around the docks is a great area as congested and overcrowded in parts as the river-side areas of south

and east London. The vast population does not trouble 'the churches', nor scarcely is it troubled by the churches. It is true that there are popular down-town churches, frankly, recruited from suburbia.

The areas surrounding the new hall presents a tragic problem of human listlessness and indifference to the best things in life.

Methodism has accepted the challenge of the dockland's need, believing that in her genius for winning the masses to Christ she has in Southampton an open door of opportunity.

The Methodist congregation's vision for Central Hall was ambitious and comprehensive. When the building was constructed in the early 1920s, a sign outside read, 'Workers Wanted with Grace, Grit and Gumption', and a list of activities to be offered included sick nursing, food depots, maternity and baby care, legal advice, moral clinics, evening classes, organ recitals and more. The opening leaflet for Central Hall described the building's role as a centre of Christian service and community outreach:

Hence the Central Hall will become a busy hive of positive ideals and interests with CHRIST as the CENTRE.

Over the years, Central Hall lived up to this vision, hosting local operatic and music societies, film screenings and other community activities. It was a place of vibrant spiritual and cultural life.

The early years saw significant events, such as evangelist George Jeffreys' mission in 1927, which resulted in more than 1,000 new commitments to Christ and led to the formation of several local Elim Pentecostal churches. In 1947, Billy Graham preached his first message on English soil at Southampton Central Hall during his inaugural trip to the UK. The building also served as a venue for Youth for Christ gatherings during the 1950s and 1960s. However, by the mid-1960s, the Methodist congregation had diminished, leading to the sale of Central Hall to Hampshire County Council.

When we acquired Central Hall, it was in a rather dilapidated state, but the potential for renewal and the continuation of its mission was evident. As we embarked on the journey of restoration, it was with a sense of historical continuity and a deep appreciation for the vision that had originally inspired the construction of Central Hall. Our commitment was to build upon the legacy of the past while forging a new future for the church and the community we served.

Chapter Eleven

Adjusting to the New

The change was a significant one. Now a city centre church with a large, albeit neglected building that required a lot of work. It would take some adjusting to compared to our previous nomadic existence hiring school halls, community centres and university lecture theatres.

Potential

Our new location was far from ideal but in estate agent 'speak', it had lots of potential. The church building stood amid a barren expanse, flanked by open land and an almost derelict shopping centre. The East Street Shopping Centre had become little more than a pedestrian thoroughfare with many empty shop units, and bore the scars of vandalism on its rooftop car park. To one side of Central Hall, a small petrol station clung to relevance, while a boarded-up former school loomed on the other. Behind us lay the abandoned Chantry

Hall, a silent companion to the St Mary's Church building across the road.

Central Hall itself had suffered from years of neglect. The main auditorium had been colonised by a flock of pigeons; their presence unmistakably marked on the wooden tiled floor. Ancillary rooms echoed with emptiness, and the smaller hall had been repurposed into a two-storey painting and decorating teaching facility. The car parks to the rear and side were covered in weeds, and the doors and windows of the building were barely held together.

In the autumn of 1990, the congregation was invited to an 'introductory service' in the main hall. We were all advised to bring cushions and blankets, a clear indication of the hall's dilapidated state. This gathering was our first real look at what we had committed to, and to the extensive work required to transform it into a functional venue.

The hall was characterised by a grand, symmetrical layout with rows of dark-stained wooden seating facing a raised stage area. The stage was flanked by staircases on either side, leading up to additional seating and exits.

The ceiling of the hall was vaulted with a series of curved arches, and large rectangular skylights that once allowed natural light to filter into the space were now covered over. Ageing decorative light fixtures hung from the ceiling, contributing to the hall's elegant and somewhat solemn atmosphere. The seating was organised in a combination of lower-floor and balcony sections, separated by a 6ft-high wooden barrier, made of the same dark-stained wood as the seating.

Colin Henderson took on the monumental task of overseeing the renovation, supported by a dedicated team of craftsmen and volunteers. The priority was to replace the leaking roof and dismantle the massive organ in the main hall. Carpet tiles, salvaged from a nearby office complex that was shutting down, were laid in the main hall, corridors and ancillary rooms. Day after day, volunteers showed up to clean, paint and clear out rubbish. Second-hand kitchen equipment was purchased and installed, inching us closer to our goal.

By the early spring of 1991, the initial phase was almost complete. On Sunday, 7th April, the week after Easter Sunday, we held our first formal meeting in the newly habitable building. While further phases were planned, including roof replacements over the wings, foyer upgrades and heating installation in all ancillary rooms, we had made a significant leap forward. Our journey had begun in earnest, and we were ready to embrace the future with renewed hope.

The transition to our new, permanent home was a significant adjustment for us, marking the end of a very itinerant existence. Our journey began at the Centre for the Blind, then moved to the Gregg School on Winn Road, followed by a stint at Bitterne Park School. These locations were mere waypoints as we navigated through various phases of our church life.

The shift to 'area settings' brought another season of change, with monthly gatherings at Boldrewood becoming our new rhythm. Our 'area settings' initially expanded from four to eight, and then consolidated back to three. For the past twelve months, we had found a semblance of stability by meeting together at Boldrewood, which fostered a greater sense of unity and community as well as shared vision.

Settling in

Now, we were finally settling into our new and permanent home, together as one church under one roof. This new chapter was more than just a change of address; it was a momentous step for our church congregation, allowing us to grow and flourish together in a place we could truly call our own.

We also marked the occasion with a subtle change of name from Southampton Community Church to The Community Church, Southampton. Although, to most people we were always simply known as 'Community'.

On that first Sunday, 7th April 1991, we received a prophetic word that resonated with us all:

> As I brought you across the Jordan close to Jericho so I say to you that this is the house of faith, this is the place of Jericho where I will demonstrate my authority and power in the midst of my people . . . so I will prepare you for new areas of ministry and new areas of responsibility, for this wineskin will grow and cover much more than it does at this time.

We were excited by the possibilities that this new venue would afford us. Remembering the prophetic word, that we 'would inherit a building our forefathers had laboured for', meant we already had a good template from our Methodist forefathers as to how they envisaged Central Hall being used.

Recalling those words in the final Methodist magazine for Central Hall in 1965, that there 'may be many more chapters still to be written in which the Lord may be glorified', we anticipated fulfilling that statement.

To facilitate this new season, the leadership team also had to adapt and embrace new responsibilities for this exciting time.

There was a lot to learn for every one of us.

Tony was the senior leader, with primary responsibility to cast vision, provide direction and lead the team. But he was not a typical 'senior pastor' who was around all the time, involved in every major decision and preaching most Sundays. He continued to have a significant involvement in developing the national and international work of Cornerstone; therefore, his role was more about empowering and releasing the existing team at the church, ensuring that his broader responsibilities did not impede the local mission.

Previously, the three primary area leaders – Dave Adcock, Phil Orchard and Allan Cox – had shared similar roles, each overseeing various groups across the church: Dave in the west of the city, Phil in the east and Allan in the north. However, in this new phase, their roles were realigned to better match their unique skills and passions.

Dave took on the responsibility for communications, programming and events. Phil was appointed as the director of training, with a vision to enhance the equipping of every church member, ensuring that everyone had the tools and knowledge to grow and serve effectively. Allan embraced the role of pastoral director, focusing on creating a robust framework for pastoral care and support across the church community.

Hannah, Tony's wife, spearheaded worship and prayer, supported by Lynn Swart, a dear South African ministry friend who had been serving the church since 1987, but was now in the process of relocating to Southampton. Tony Rozee continued his coordination of evangelism, passionately driving the outreach efforts. I was once again working full-time in the church to serve our young people and students, a role close to my heart, while also supporting several churches within the Cornerstone network.

Adrian Thomas broadened his role to embrace all aspects of the church's development as business director, with Colin Henderson leading on the development and repurposing of Central Hall.

This realignment of roles and responsibilities was not just a necessary adjustment but a strategic development, positioning us to better serve our congregation and community, and to thrive in this new chapter of our church's journey.

After moving into our new facility, we eagerly began exploring the myriads of possibilities it offered.

Opportunities

Our journey started with hosting a variety of events aimed at young people. One of our first initiatives was an alternative worship event called God's Own, later renamed Outhouse. This unique gathering featured a dynamic blend of DJ-led worship, captivating visuals and artistic expressions, creating an immersive and spiritually enriching experience.

Central Hall also became the home for Radio Cracker, a charity radio station, for three weeks over the 1991 Christmas period, operated entirely by volunteers and focused on raising funds for various charitable projects around the world. This was part of a wider nationwide project initiated by Steve Chalke's Oasis charity.

In the summer of 1992, we had the privilege of hosting a Youth With A Mission (YWAM) team for two weeks of outreach activities based in the building. This period of intense outreach culminated in a groundbreaking event, a 'rave in the nave', which drew hundreds of unchurched young people, providing them with a memorable and impacting encounter.

We formed a strategic partnership with New Generation Ministries from Bristol, who provided one of their youth outreach bands for a whole year. Together, we organised regular events and school ministry programmes, engaging and inspiring the youth in our community.

Recognising the diverse needs of our congregation, we also focused on the older generation. Colin and Brenda Henderson, with a dedicated team, initiated an outreach programme for senior citizens called Sunday Afternoon at Central Hall. This monthly gathering quickly became a beloved event, attracting more than 100 attendees each time. The programme featured familiar hymns, heartfelt testimonies and engaging topics, followed by a delightful afternoon tea, creating a warm and welcoming atmosphere for all.

Christmas provided us with a remarkable opportunity to highlight the musical and artistic talents within our church, making it an ideal occasion to invite family and friends to hear and experience the message of Christ's birth. Penny Hastings, a gifted musician and music teacher, along with Gill Escott, a former professional dancer with the Royal Ballet, led the creative team. Their combined expertise resulted in spectacular events that became so popular we had to run them over two nights each year to meet the high demand for tickets.

These festive celebrations also marked the inception of the Central Hall Community Choir, which went on to perform and enrich our community for many years to come.

Sunday mornings

Our weekly Sunday morning gatherings experienced a period of significant growth, with many new people coming to see what was happening at Central Hall. This influx of attendees highlighted the exceptional quality of our musicians and singers who formed the worship team. The freedom and dynamism of Spirit-led worship had been a hallmark of our church since the very beginning, and the new building provided a platform – both literally and figuratively – for this vibrant expression of faith. There are many stories of people attending Central Hall for the first time and being deeply moved by the worship they encountered.

Preaching was conducted on a rotational basis. At that time, we did not follow a sermon series or teaching plan. Instead, those scheduled to speak would seek God, receive his guidance and deliver the message that God had laid on their hearts. There was always an opportunity for response, and a team was available to pray for all those who came forward.

Maggie Orchard, a primary school teacher by profession, took on the responsibility of developing our children's ministry. Her husband, Phil, in his role as director of training, created a comprehensive twenty-week midweek training programme called the Equipping Programme. Additionally, he developed an existing three-year course titled Handle With Care, which provided an in-depth study of Christian doctrine over that extended period.

Our Crossroads telephone helpline continued to support many individuals in crisis. Over time, it expanded to include a dedicated line for young people, called Teenline, offering specialised assistance to the younger members of our community.

Allan and Lizzie Cox were busy developing a pastoral team to help support the members of the congregation, helping them feel connected and cared for in the new environment.

With all this new growth and expansion, the decision was also made to reduce our involvement with The King's School Senior, which continued to meet at the Fisher's Pond site. It was becoming an increasingly heavy financial burden, and many of the families from the church who had sent their children to The King's Primary School had chosen not to send them to the senior school. After careful consideration and prayer, the leadership concluded that our vision was for primary education only, allowing us to lay solid foundations in the lives of our children. They decided that this vision did not extend to secondary education, which requires more expertise and much better facilities and resources.

Additionally, we were encouraging people in the church to engage with their local communities, recognising that the school gate is one of the best places to meet others in the community. Many of the church members had embraced this challenge and were getting involved with local schools and community groups.

However, a group of parents and teachers involved with The King's School at Fisher's Pond expressed their desire to continue with secondary education, which led to the formation of a new charitable trust, Hampshire Christian Education Trust, to operate the secondary school element of The King's School at the site. The church, who owned the site with Eastleigh Christian Fellowship, agreed to allow the new school to operate at the Fisher's Pond site for up to five years.

And so, in September 1992, ten years after the opening of The King's School in West End, The King's School Senior reopened officially under the governance of the Hampshire Christian Education Trust, with Paul Trevett appointed as headteacher.

This period from 1990 onwards coincided with the Church of England's Decade of Evangelism, an ambitious initiative launched by the Anglican Church and spearheaded by the Archbishop of Canterbury, George Carey. The primary goal of this initiative was to renew and energise the Church's commitment to evangelism and mission work in response to declining church attendance and the increasing secularisation of society.

During this time, various evangelistic initiatives were introduced, including the Jesus in Me campaign. This initiative aimed to emphasise the personal relationship individuals can have with Jesus Christ and to encourage people to explore and deepen their faith. It was designed to make the Christian faith more accessible and relatable by focusing on personal experiences and testimonies.

Simultaneously, the seeker-sensitive services pioneered by Willow Creek Community Church in Chicago were gaining widespread attention in the UK. These services, designed to make church more accessible to non-believers, involved a contemporary approach to worship and preaching. Recognising the potential of these methods, Dave Adcock and Adrian Thomas travelled to Chicago to witness the Willow Creek model firsthand. They returned profoundly impacted by their experience and began contemplating how to implement similar strategies at Central Hall.

The whole Church in the UK, including our own, was mobilising for evangelistic mission. We recognised the urgent need to extend our reach beyond our immediate community. With our newly acquired building, we consciously decided against defaulting to a large, attractional model of church. Although the sheer presence of our spacious city centre church was naturally drawing people – many already Christians from across the city – our true mission was to connect with those who had no prior church experience or faith in Christ.

What happened next took us all somewhat by surprise.

Chapter Twelve

Toronto

The 26th June 1994 is a date that will forever be remembered as a milestone in the history of The Community Church, Southampton.

Students

Two weeks prior, I had attended a meeting with our student group on Sunday evening, 12th June. The group, led by Storm Drew, our student coordinator, had been attracting a considerable number of students. Storm had informed me that there was a fresh move of the Holy Spirit taking place at their Sunday evening meetings. Intrigued and somewhat sceptical, I decided to go and witness it for myself.

I was utterly blown away by what I experienced. This is what I wrote in my journal that evening:

> Went along to the student prayer meeting this evening. Amazing scenes. People drunk in the Holy Spirit, laughing uncontrollably, weeping, moaning, falling over. What a remarkable change in this quiet, reserved, and rational student group.

What I had just experienced was remarkably like the John Wimber event that I had attended in 1984. But now it was happening here in Southampton.

Storm asked if the group could meet in one of the rooms at Central Hall rather than at her home. We agreed, and so the following Sunday, the meeting took place in Room 4, one of our larger ancillary rooms. The meeting on 19th June attracted an unusually high number of students. Crammed into Room 4, I once again witnessed what was nothing short of miraculous as everyone present was reaching out to God in worship and ministering to each other. There was a dynamic move of the Holy Spirit.

I shared with the other church leaders what I had experienced, and we decided to highlight what was happening at the next Sunday morning meeting, 26th June.

As that Sunday approached there was a growing sense of anticipation. Tony Rozee was scheduled to preach. He shared some stories he had heard about this fresh move of the Holy Spirit beginning to impact churches across the UK and he also talked about what had been happening in the student group. He concluded his talk with a simple prayer of invitation for those who wanted to receive a fresh impartation of the Holy

Spirit. Tony Morton was present that Sunday and joined Tony Rozee on the platform, endorsing his appeal.

Before anyone could respond, a young student seated in the front row began to laugh uncontrollably. Slowly, the laughter spread to others around her, then across the entire room. People began to come forward, some weeping, some shaking, some falling to the floor after receiving prayer. Others stood by, watching in awe, others somewhat confused. Despite the apparent chaos, there was an incredible sense of God's peaceful presence in the room. Even the children and young people, returning from their activities, were struck by the extraordinary atmosphere that seemed chaotic but felt divinely ordered.

Everyone

It was announced that the student group meeting scheduled for that evening would relocate to the main hall and be open to anyone interested in finding out more. That evening, ninety people showed up, equivalent to a full 20 per cent of the church at that time.

Within four weeks, despite most students returning home for the summer, the Sunday evening gatherings were drawing 250 people from across the city and the wider region, all hungry to experience this fresh move of the Holy Spirit.

This new wave of Holy Spirit activity could be traced back to some extraordinary events in Toronto at the Airport Vineyard church in January 1994. John and Carol Arnott, the pastors, had served faithfully for many years but felt something was lacking in their ministry. In the autumn of 1993, the Arnotts travelled to Argentina, which had been experiencing revival since 1984. There, they were prayed for by two influential leaders of the Argentine revival, Claudio Freidzon and Carlos Annacondia. Following their prayers, the Arnotts returned to Canada, and within a few months, the fresh move of the Holy Spirit started.

Randy Clark, who was pastoring a Vineyard church in St Louis, Missouri, experienced a dramatic renewal in his own life and in his church. This renewal was highly influenced by the ministry of Rodney Howard-Browne, a South African preacher.

Arnott, inspired by Clark's testimony of personal renewal, invited him to preach at the Toronto Airport Vineyard church over the weekend of 20th-23rd January 1994.

At the end of the service on 20th January, with about 120 people in attendance, virtually the entire congregation responded to the invitation for prayer. What ensued was a wide range of manifestations, including laughter, falling, prostration, and what was later referred to as being 'drunk in the Spirit'. Some experienced visions and intense conviction of sin and spiritual transformation.

Arnott persuaded Clark to stay and continue preaching, which he did for about sixty days, finally returning to his own congregation in mid-March. During these first few months, the Toronto church's regular attendance tripled to more than 1,000 as the revival's influence spread. Reports of similar outpourings began to emerge globally, sparked by the events in Toronto. Visitors from other cities and nations carried the revival's influence back to their home congregations, perpetuating the revival in their own churches.

By May 1994, the revival had spread to England as leaders from several churches travelled to Toronto to witness the events firsthand. One such leader was Eleanor Mumford of the South West London Vineyard church. Dramatically influenced by the Holy Spirit during her visit, Mumford was invited to speak at Holy Trinity Brompton, a prestigious Anglican church, on 29th May 1994. After sharing her testimony, similar manifestations occurred at HTB.

This pattern was repeated across many churches in the United Kingdom from late May onwards, in what has now been termed the 'Toronto Blessing'.

A fresh move

People around the world reported an almost identical, unscripted pattern of manifestations that characterised this fresh move, including:

> **A profound consciousness of God:** One of the most significant manifestations was a sense of the awesome presence of God. The Baptist author Henry Blackaby states in his blog that this is common in most genuine revivals, as it severely convicts of sin and leads people to genuine repentance. This presence also brought

joy, peace, and an awareness of God's nearness, often sensed for days by attendees.

Joy: Uncontrollable and contagious laughter was not uncommon.

Teeth filled with silver or gold: More than 300 visitors to the Toronto Airport Vineyard church claimed to have supernaturally received gold or silver fillings in their teeth during the meetings, and this was reflected in other churches around the world, including the UK.

Trembling of the body: As reported in many historic revivals, physical spasms involving trembling or shaking occurred, referred to in previous generations as paroxysms or 'the jerks'.

Loss of physical strength: Many people lost physical strength due to the presence of God, often unable to rise from the ground for hours.

Spiritual 'drunkenness': Some were unable to walk in a straight line or even stand.

Weeping: Many wept inconsolably due to grief over sins, grace and mercy received, or concern for unsaved loved ones.

Spiritual power: Many testified to feeling a surge of what felt like electrical power during prayer, leading to weakness or falling to the ground, unable to maintain physical strength.

By September 1994, more than 4,000 pastors, spouses and leaders from around the world had visited the Toronto Airport church. It was estimated that by this time, as many as 3,000 churches globally had been affected.

The birth of Cutting Edge

In the first half of 1994, we had made several strategic decisions that, looking back, enabled us to make the most of this new season of refreshing we had just entered.

One of the most remarkable moments came when we hosted a youth outreach event called Interface, in our Small Hall early in the year, featuring a young worship leader named Martin Smith, along with several talented musicians from his home church in Littlehampton, a town around forty miles to the east of Southampton.

The event was nothing short of extraordinary. The palpable sense of God's presence was almost overwhelming, creating an atmosphere charged with spiritual intensity. Martin, who had recently started writing his own worship songs, brought a unique freshness to the music, coupled with a strong prophetic edge that resonated deeply with everyone present.

I remember being profoundly moved during the worship. At one point, as I looked at Martin leading the worship, I saw an immense angelic figure with outstretched arms standing behind him. This vision took my breath away. In awe, I asked the Lord, 'Who is this?' and I distinctly heard him reply, 'This is one of my angels who draws worship from the hearts of my people.' I realised then that I was witnessing something truly special and divinely orchestrated.

Following the event, we convened a meeting with Martin and his keyboard player, Tim Jupp, to discuss the possibility of organising a regular youth worship event at Central Hall. They had been running a monthly event at their home church in Littlehampton called Cutting Edge and felt a calling to expand their reach.

We had recently formed a partnership with City Gate Church and a newly established Vineyard church, both in Southampton, to host the Interface event, which was a youth outreach initiative similar in style and spirit to Cutting Edge. As we discussed and prayed over the proposal, it became clear that we should seize the opportunity to host a monthly Cutting Edge event starting in September.

I remember being in a small, yet-to-be-decorated room in the caretaker's flat at Central Hall. There, I gathered with Tim, Martin, Kevin Allan, leader of City Gate Church, Steve Lee, evangelist and member of City Gate Church, and Matt Hyam, leader of the Southampton Vineyard group. We discussed and prayed earnestly about the potential partnership. On the table in the centre of the room was a tray of coffee cups. I arranged the cups so their rims touched each other, then picked up a jug of water and began pouring into the central cup. As the central cup overflowed, it began to fill the other cups, creating a visual representation of what I sensed God wanted to do through the Cutting Edge event – impacting and filling many other contexts with his presence.

Alpha

The second decision we had already made was that we were going to launch an Alpha course at the beginning of 1995.

In early 1994, HTB, a major catalyst for the Toronto Blessing and located in the heart of London, hosted an Alpha training event that Phil Orchard attended. HTB, renowned for its vibrant worship and innovative approach to ministry, had been the birthplace of the Alpha course – a practical introduction to the Christian faith designed primarily for non-churchgoers and new Christians.

The Alpha course was originally developed in 1977 by Charles Marnham, a curate at HTB, as a short course for new Christians. However, it was under the leadership of Nicky Gumbel, a former barrister who had joined the church staff, that Alpha truly began to flourish. Gumbel recognised the course's potential to reach a broader audience and started to rework the material into a series of talks that could engage and inspire seekers and sceptics alike.

The training event held in early 1994 was a concentrated effort to equip church leaders and laypeople with the tools and understanding needed to run their own Alpha courses. This event marked a significant turning point, as it aimed to expand the reach of Alpha beyond the walls of HTB and into churches across the UK and eventually the world.

Attendees from various denominations gathered to learn about the vision and practicalities of Alpha. They participated in workshops that covered the essentials of running an Alpha course, from organising small group discussions to creating a welcoming environment for guests. The training emphasised the importance of hospitality, open dialogue and the power of the Holy Spirit in transforming lives.

Nicky Gumbel and his team passionately conveyed the core principles of Alpha, highlighting its focus on the basics of Christianity: Who is Jesus? Why did Jesus die? How can we have faith? Why and how do I pray? The sessions were designed to be engaging, accessible and relatable, breaking down complex theological concepts into digestible conversations.

One of the standout moments of the event was the emphasis on the role of the Holy Spirit. Gumbel shared testimonies of how Alpha had been a conduit for people to experience God's presence in profound and life-changing ways. The training included sessions on praying for guests and creating opportunities for them to encounter the Holy Spirit during the course.

Attendees, including our own Phil Orchard, left inspired and equipped to start Alpha courses in their own communities. The simplicity and relational approach of Alpha made it adaptable and appealing to a wide range of cultural contexts.

Cell groups

In addition to this, we had been influenced by Ralph Neighbour's book, *Where Do We Go from Here?*[5] The book challenged conventional models of church organisation, advocating for a shift from programme-centric to people-centric frameworks.

As we were working out how to be 'big church' it was helpful to read about his approach to decentralised, member-led structures that fostered a much greater sense of shared responsibility and collaborative ministry among members of the congregation.

Neighbour's advocacy for small, intimate groups – referred to as 'cells' – as the fundamental units of church life, found fertile ground in our church and in many churches across the UK. The cell groups were focused on fostering close-knit communities where members could engage deeply with their faith, support one another and participate actively in ministry. This was how our church began, and Neighbour's emphasis enabled us to see how we could do both 'big' and 'small' at the same time.

And so, in the autumn of 1994, we were set to launch 'neighbourhood groups' based on Ralph Neighbour's cell church model.

This fresh vision for small groups, our decision to host Cutting Edge youth events, and plans for the launch of the Alpha course pre-dated 26th June but that day began to add 'fuel to the fire' and our commitment to fulfil God's purposes for our city.

Looking forward

In November, Tony Morton summarised things in the end-of-year Looking Forward document:

The Holy Spirit has come among us in a refreshing and surprising way over recent months. We are privileged to be experiencing his power in new ways. Let us keep asking for more!

These are days of refreshing and adjustment. We have taken many practical steps, such as refurbishing the Small Hall, now with a new floor and heating, but these practical steps are only fulfilling as we see it used to help hundreds discover Jesus and his risen power.

Let's keep our eyes fixed on being a growing happy Christian community and enjoy the adventure on the way. We have a city and a world to reach with the message of hope and power which Jesus brings.

Changes are ahead of us. A change of focus and shape for our small groups, new strategies to communicate the reality of Jesus to our friends, and new opportunities to help serve the vision. Challenges and surprises await us as we stand and move together.

Announcing a new strategy for monthly 'Tithe Sundays', Tony also shared:

> For four years our church finances have focused on Central Hall but now it's time for a change of emphasis.
>
> 'Communicating Jesus to the world' is a key aspect of our mission statement. We hope 1995 will see a number of projects grow and develop including our new Alpha courses, the French mission base, and our work among

students and young people. Our intention is to commit more resources to the extension of the Kingdom both in this country and abroad

December the 4th will be our first 'Tithe Sunday' – a time to challenge our level of giving. In the midst of a move of God's Spirit, it's a good time to pray and reconsider.

Chapter Thirteen

Cutting Edge

In anticipation of launching the Cutting Edge events, we organised what was to be a transformative residential week for our young people in the summer of 1994.

Youth camp

We had been introduced to a group of dynamic young people from Harvest Christian Church in Port Elizabeth, South Africa. They had a thriving youth church and their vibrant faith and energy were contagious, so we invited them to lead our 'And Now This' youth camp at an activities centre near Swanage, Dorset that August. Their presence was a breath of fresh air. Like us, they had experienced a powerful move of the Holy Spirit earlier that year. They arrived brimming with faith, anticipation and a sense of purpose.

At the camp, a broad group of young people gathered, some from church families and others from outside church circles. The South African team ministered with a unique blend of passion, authenticity and fun. By the end of the week, many young people had experienced deep and transformative encounters with God, characterised by heartfelt repentance, new-found salvation and the rededication of their lives to God.

Returning to Central Hall the following Sunday, Gavin, the leader of the South African group, addressed the congregation. He recounted the extraordinary experiences of the past week and urged us all to cultivate 'open hearts, open homes and open fridges' to support these young people in their spiritual growth. He emphasised that they had been forever changed.

Up until that point, the young people typically sat at the back of the tiered seating on the right-hand side of the stage in Central Hall. Midway through his talk, Gavin asked them to stand and move across the room, finding new seats as a symbolic gesture of the change that had taken place. They rose as one and moved to the block of seats on the left-hand side of the stage, a section our young people and students would occupy for many years to come.

The first event

Having witnessed a dramatic move of God among the university students, followed by a fresh outpouring among our younger members, we eagerly prepared for the first Cutting Edge event in Southampton on Friday, 30th September. There was a tangible sense of excitement and expectation among everyone planning to attend.

Several people from Southampton had been aware of the growing popularity of the Cutting Edge events along the south coast in Littlehampton. These events had started the previous year at Arun Community Church, Littlehampton, organised by youth leaders Becca Jupp and Stew Smith in order to gather young people in the area.

The Cutting Edge Band had now formed, featuring founding members Stew Smith, Tim Jupp and Martin Smith, supported by other musicians and singers, including Stu Garrard on lead guitar, Jussy McLean on backing vocals and Les Driscoll on bass. Known for their relevant and contemporary Christian music with a strong prophetic edge, the band had already started to attract a dedicated following. Their first cassette tape of new songs, aptly entitled *Cutting Edge 1*, was being distributed, and the music spread like wildfire. The events had become more than just a concert; they were an opportunity for a deep encounter with God. Central Hall in Southampton was now poised to become a new focal point for these celebrations.

At the inaugural event, just over 150 young people gathered. Becca Jupp, the organiser of the Cutting Edge events in Littlehampton, hosted the evening and delivered a brief, impactful talk in the middle. Flanking her talk, Martin and the band introduced a host of new songs, such as 'Lord, You Have My Heart', 'The Happy Song', and 'I Could Sing of Your Love Forever', along with familiar tunes like 'His Banner Over Me Is Love'.

These songs, particularly the new ones, provided a vocabulary for a new generation, carrying a prophetic message emerging from the current move of the Holy Spirit.

By the autumn of 1994, our Sunday evening student group meetings had evolved into whole church 'refreshing meetings', attracting more than 200 people every Sunday. These gatherings were simple, often featuring a single guitar and singer, a short talk and an extended time for ministry that could last two or three hours.

Although different in style from the Cutting Edge events, these meetings were infused with the same Spirit at work.

The Cutting Edge events continued monthly until June 1995. We had been hosting them on the last Friday of each month. The Cutting Edge team would then run a similar event the next day in Portsmouth and complete their weekend back in their hometown of Littlehampton.

The band had now released their second cassette tape, *Cutting Edge 2*, and throughout the year had been introducing several new songs that would become anthems for this emerging generation, including 'Did You Feel the Mountains Tremble?' and 'I've Found Jesus'.

We took time to review whether to continue or not for another season. For us, we really sensed that God was at work. The numbers attending the final gathering in June were around 400. In May, we had begun a weekly youth congregation called Sublime that was attracting around 100 young people. We had launched Youth Alpha in a local secondary school and were witnessing many young people committing their lives to Christ. For us, the monthly Cutting Edge event created the focal point for all that was happening, and we were keen to continue. The two other churches involved with us at this stage had decided that they could not be as involved because of other commitments, and the responsibility to continue therefore rested with us.

The Cutting Edge team were happy to continue with their monthly commitment. They decided that they would move the event from a Friday to a Saturday, stop hosting in Portsmouth, but continue their regular Sunday evening event in Littlehampton.

During the summer, Martin, the lead singer of the band, was involved in a serious road accident and spent several weeks in hospital. It was during this time that he decided now was the time to dedicate himself to becoming a full-time musician.

September came quickly. With the closure of the event in Portsmouth (approximately half an hour away by car), numbers swelled to around 600 and grew each month. The event also grew in quality, both technically and musically. The band were now on the high stage at Central Hall, a new lighting rig had been hired, Martin was still with his leg in plaster, and had Stu Garrard and Jon Thatcher join the line-up permanently. The event also grew in spiritual intensity, with many testifying to deep encounters with God during the worship and in the times of response.

In January 1996, the band adopted the name Delirious? and began to operate as full-time musicians.

Outdoors

In June, at the end of the second year of events, we decided to host the Cutting Edge event outdoors in Hoglands Park, just across the road from Central Hall. Some 1,500 people turned up.

As a whole church, we were now attending the Springbank Bible weekend in Essex over the May bank holiday each year. The newly named Delirious? band were invited to lead worship, and the Sublime leadership team hosted all youth activities. It was a powerful time and introduced the songs and passion of the Cutting Edge events to a much wider audience.

By this time, *Cutting Edge 3* and *Cutting Edge 4* cassette tapes had been released, and the reach of the music was now becoming global.

In September 1996, we launched our third, and what was to be our final year of Cutting Edge events. So many people attended the first event that September, there was a long queue around the building. The following month we had to turn people away because we were at capacity. One coachload of young people had travelled from Bristol and were unable to gain entrance. It was decided that we would need to make use of tickets for health and safety purposes, and to avoid future disappointment.

Tickets would sell out as soon as they were released. Our capacity was 1,200, and each month the main hall would now be full. The spiritual intensity and expectation were so high. Every month, hundreds of young people would respond to the call to salvation and rededication. Many more had fresh encounters with God, with numerous reports of healing and spiritual breakthrough.

We were planning to host an end-of-year outdoor event again and considered using the Southampton Football Club stadium, called The Dell. One of my co-workers, Phil Bagge, and I were looking at this option and together we were watching *Match of the Day* one Saturday evening. It was Saturday, 26th October 1996, and Southampton rather unexpectedly beat Manchester United 6-3 at The Dell. At the end of the game, the commentator made the statement, 'And The Dell has gone delirious!' We almost fell off our chairs and took it as a sign that we should approach the club.

We did contact the club but were informed it was not possible to hire the stadium at the end of the season, but 1998 might be a possibility. We therefore concluded the series of events in June 1997 with another outdoor event in Hoglands Park, which attracted more than 3,000 people.

By this time, the band Delirious? had released their first album, *King of Fools*, and were touring extensively. We sadly concluded that the outdoor event in Hoglands Park would be our final Cutting Edge event. But we did agree that we would continue monthly events with our own team of musicians from Sublime, our youth congregation, which we would call the Big Story.

So, in September of that year, 1997, at the Southampton Guildhall, Delirious? as part of their national tour, were supported by the Sublime musicians, and the Big Story was launched.

The Dell

These were heady days. It wasn't just the monthly Cutting Edge events that were amazing but everything around those events. The birth and growth of the Sublime youth congregation; Youth Alpha running in secondary schools across the city; Cutting Edge mission teams to Canada, Ireland, Germany, South Africa and Colombia; the launch of the Big Story; the development of youth cells; the formation of the sub:city dance outreach team . . . and then The Dell '98!

We did go back to the football club and enquire about hiring the stadium for an event at the end of the 1997-98 season. Much to our surprise, they agreed. Keith Bryan, a former police officer who had recently moved to Southampton, offered to take responsibility for the organisation. He did a fantastic job in pulling everything together, from staging, PA, visuals, booking artists, and setting up a ticketing system.

And so, on Friday, 8th May 1998, we hosted The Dell '98 Spiritual Gathering. In the introduction of the programme, I wrote:

The Road to The Dell

Four years ago, some people discussed the possibility of running an event in Southampton called Cutting Edge.

This was a worship event for young people that was already proving to be a winning formula in Littlehampton. So, in October 1994, the Cutting Edge event began with 150 people. More and more young people started to attend, experiencing the passion and depth that was there. In 1996, the worship band changed their name to Delirious? and we began to talk about the possibility of The Dell. In June last year, just over 3,000 attended the open-air Cutting Edge event in the heart of Southampton, and The Dell was now in sight. This last year has been spent planning, negotiating, and trying to find the best approach to an event of this size.

We hope you enjoy the evening, are challenged by it, and experience spiritual renewal as you encounter Jesus, the living God.

More than 6,000 people purchased tickets.

Paul Woodman, an evangelist based in the city, and Caz Britten, a member of the sub:city dance team, had spent weeks working in schools across the city, inviting young people. We had so much support from local churches, many of whom agreed to underwrite the venture with us.

One disappointment was that, because of tour commitments, the Delirious? guys were unable to do a full set. They did, however, appear and do a smaller acoustic set. But with support from New Generation Ministries, Soul Survivor, The Message and local artists, we had a great line-up.

DJ Santer, a local Christian student worker and DJ, got things started and was accompanied by our in-house sub:city dance team. The NGM band, Steve, then played a set, followed by Matt Redman, the worship leader from Soul Survivor. Hydro, a dance duet from Bristol, were up next and the Worldwide Message Tribe from Manchester 'topped the bill'.

We also had spoken contributions from our very own Tony Morton, Greg Valerio, social justice campaigner, and two young people from the church, Rachel Orchard and Pete Williams.

It was a fantastic event and one of the final non-football events hosted at The Dell before the football club moved to their new stadium in 2001.

I did wonder if this would be the start of a new phase of ministry for us a church but as I reflected, I felt that what The Dell '98 did was bring a conclusion to a season of ministry rather than the start of a new one.

The Cutting Edge events had a significant impact on young people in our church, across the city and even further afield. We had seen the birth of our youth congregation, Sublime, now led by Dave Boniface, the launch of the Big Story that would continue to attract hundreds of young people, mission teams and outreach teams serving across the city and the nations.

But most importantly the greatest impact was in the lives of the hundreds and hundreds of young people who had encountered God in fresh ways and would go on to be, as the Delirious? song loudly proclaimed, 'History Maker[s]'!

A catalyst for the next generation

What was happening in Southampton was also being mirrored in many other parts of the country with an increasing fruitfulness among young people. Revelation Church in Chichester had launched a youth church, as had New Generation Ministries in Bristol. Soul Survivor was attracting thousands of young people and had recently planted the Soul

Survivor Church in Watford. Delirious? were touring the country making lots of new connections. We decided to form a group and host a series of conferences to explore 'church in youth culture'. These ran from 1996 to 1998 under the name Remix and from 1999 to 2001 with the name Cultural Shift.

These were formative times for many of us with a strong prophetic call to the next generation. The conference at our own Central Hall in 1999 was particularly significant in that it was the catalyst for the launch of the 24-7 prayer movement. Pete Greig tells the story in his book, *Red Moon Rising*:

> As we gathered on that cold November night in 1999, Central Hall was heaving with people dancing to DJ Andy Hunter's mix of heavenly beats. So many people were being impacted by the 24-7 prayer rooms in Sidcup and Chichester that we had decided to establish one for the weekend here too. Suddenly Roger Ellis, the ex-head-banger from Chichester, came bounding up to me looking extremely excited. In his usual croaky growl he said, 'Pete, maybe we could fill a whole year with unbroken prayer.' I looked nervous but Roger was, by now, bouncing around with excitement: 'Maybe people want to try this 24-7 prayer thing back home for a week or more. If everyone did a week we could link it all together and fill the year 2000! What do you think?' It had taken Roger about ten seconds to download an idea that would take the rest of us the rest of our lives to outwork.

On the Sunday morning, we moved the conference from Central Hall into a cavernous local nightclub. A matter of hours earlier, the place had been jammed with Saturday night party people, drinking, dancing and flirting. And so, as we entered the building to worship and pray, the air was still stale from the night before.

As the morning progressed, I climbed onto a podium usually occupied by the best, or most scantily clad, dancers. I didn't quite measure up to either of these criteria with my scruffy T-shirt and gangly frame, but right now the podium was a pulpit and I had a proposal to make.

'If anyone wants to pray non-stop for a week or more with their friends next year, let me know afterwards,' I said, looking dubiously down at the dusky crowd on the circular dance floor. 'Maybe we could fill the whole of next year with prayer.' A cheer of approval rose from the floor and in a flush of enthusiasm I would soon regret, I added, 'We'll try and hook it all up online.' Everyone cheered once again.

I jumped down from my pulpit to discover that we had, effectively, just launched a prayer movement. People began to hand me contact details indicating their intention to pray non-stop for a significant chunk of the year 2000. The prayer virus that had been incubating with increasing intensity in our Chichester warehouse had found its first willing carriers in this Southampton nightclub. The epidemic had well and truly begun.[6]

The group at Dales Bible Week 1977

An early Bible Week, circa 1983. L-R Pete Fung,
Roger Popplestone, Ken Ford, Larry Tomczak, Arthur Wallis

The church elders praying for Jean Kalmier as she heads to Nepal
as a missionary 1983. L-R Arthur Wallis, Phil Clarke, Mick Caws,
Geoff Wright, Roger Popplestone, Tony Morton, Mike Evans

Bible Weeks circa 1984

Baptisms circa 1986

King's School 1987

Cutting Edge worship band
[pre-Delirious?] circa 1995

Crowds waiting to get in to the
Cutting Edge event circa 1996

Gathering at The Dell 1998

Crowds at The Dell

The Dell '98 brochure

Worship team at Central Hall circa 2002 L-R Luke Strickland, Sarah Amer, Dave Lee, Lynn Swart, Jonathan Cathie, John Mowforth

Transition of leadership 2002

Final c.net meeting 2004

Central Hall post-refurbishment circa 2009. Caroline Kennedy speaking

Under construction circa 1924

The original hall circa 1930

Central Hall circa 1930

First Pioneer conference at Central Hall 2010

Those who attended the very first meeting in 1975 still part of the church in 2015 – 40 years on

Interview with the DfE for Hope Community School 2014

Opening of Oasis Academy with local dignatories September 2012

Our house in France – New Community Le Vay circa 2015

Leadership transition to Theo and Sarah Amer October 2022

Transition weekend 2022

The Hope Bell in Southampton's historic Bargate

Chapter Fourteen

A Weaving of Ministries

During the mid to late nineties, there were a lot of other activities and developments taking place across the church, beyond our work with young people. Many were being added to us, weaving together a beautiful mix of ministries and resources.

Ministry developments

Phil Orchard had assembled a dedicated team and launched Alpha, the course designed for seekers and new Christians, developed by Nicky Gumbel and the team at HTB, as previously mentioned. Over the first four years, we hosted twelve ten-week courses, attracting close to 350 participants. The enthusiasm and commitment of the team were palpable, making a significant impact on many lives.

Allan Cox, in his role as pastoral director, identified a critical need for a counselling resource to support those in our congregation with more complex psychological needs. At that time, only a few people were receiving the psychological help they needed, and those who did had to afford private fees for the required therapeutic services.

Recognising this gap, we invited Norma Parrack, a highly trained counsellor and a valued member of The Community Church, to establish the Central Counselling Service. This service provided affordable, professional therapeutic support for the church community, with additional bursaries available for those facing financial difficulties. Operating from Central Hall, the service quickly grew, expanding its offerings to include training for counsellors alongside its counselling services. This expansion led to a rebranding as the Central Counselling and Training Service, or CCTS for short.

CCTS flourished, providing counselling to thousands in the Southampton area for nearly three decades. A substantial number of new counsellors were trained through CCTS, many of whom went on to establish similar services in Edinburgh, Bournemouth and the New Forest, as well as starting their own practices. CCTS offered ongoing support to these new centres and individuals with supervision and ongoing professional development training.

Dave Adcock continued his mission in France, forging strong connections with Christians in Normandy. In 1995, we secured an agreement with a Christian homeowner in the region to use their home as a base for our teams travelling to France. These teams regularly visited to pray, meet local Christians and support local churches, developing meaningful cross-cultural friendships.

Tony Rozee, who had been leading our evangelistic outreaches, had accepted the invitation to become leader of the New Forest Community Church, which had been planted by our church in the mid-1980s. He and his wife, Denise, relocated to Ashurst in the New Forest to take on this new responsibility.

In 1994, we also made the significant decision to sell Foulis Court at Fisher's Pond, which had been home to The King's School Senior for just under five years. The school relocated to a new site a few miles away on Allington Lane in Fair Oak, situated on the edge of the city.

New additions

The year 1996 brought key individuals who significantly strengthened the church's ministry as an apostolic resource church. Graham Cooke, a nationally and internationally recognised prophetic minister, joined us following the unfortunate split of his previous church in Southampton. His deep involvement in prophetic ministry brought a new dimension to our church.

Peter Butt, a church leader from Essex with a growing teaching ministry, also joined us. Having felt a strong calling through prophetic words, he and his wife, Irene, moved to Southampton in 1996, further enriching our community.

Steve Lee, an itinerant evangelist, faced a similar dilemma to Graham Cooke during the leadership difficulties at his previous church. After knowing and working with Steve for several years, I was delighted when he and his wife, Lorraine, and their family decided to join The Community Church in 1997.

It was fascinating to see how God wove together each of these individuals and their families, bringing them together to be a part of the church. They each added depth and variety of ministry that we didn't even realise we needed.

As an apostolic community, we always had a vision that extended beyond our local parish or area. We knew we were called to impact the city, the nation and the nations. The planting of churches in the region, the development of the Cornerstone Network, connections with an increasing number of nations and the development of training programmes confirmed that this was indeed our God-given calling.

And we now had a very clear physical presence in the city in the shape of Central Hall that provided opportunities for events and conferences to serve the wider Church.

Redevelopment

Over time, the area surrounding Central Hall underwent significant redevelopment. The once almost derelict East Street shopping centre was sold, paving the way for developers to propose new plans for its transformation. Meanwhile, the Old Deanery school was demolished, making room for the construction of a modern block of student accommodation for the newly established Solent University. The petrol station, after struggling for a few years, was eventually sold, with subsequent plans drawn up for a mixed-use development comprising both private and social housing. Chantry Hall, a building we had once considered acquiring, was ultimately demolished following a brief stint as a nightclub and a mysterious fire. Across St Mary Street, the vacant land was similarly revitalised, leading to the development of additional student accommodation.

This redevelopment around Central Hall had a significant impact on the mission of the church. With the new student accommodation and housing developments, the area saw an influx of new residents, particularly young people. This presented an opportunity for the church to expand our outreach, especially towards students at Solent University. As the area around Central Hall developed and became more populated, the church's location proved to be central and accessible. This increased visibility and drew in more visitors, making it easier for the church to become a hub for community activities and events.

Songs of Praise

Songs of Praise is a long-running religious television programme broadcast every Sunday by the BBC. It is one of the most popular and enduring religious shows on British television, known for its format of featuring hymns and spiritual songs, alongside stories of faith and inspirational interviews.

It was much to our surprise, therefore, when we were contacted by the BBC to be asked whether we could host a *Songs of Praise* programme at Central Hall. We agreed and helped shape the programme to reflect who we were as a church community.

The programme was filmed over three days and broadcast in April 1996. The episode was hosted by a youthful Steve Chalke, who introduced the programme and the church as 'a congregation with a new love for worship, a school with a new approach to education, and a church with a new approach to mission'.[7]

The episode opened with the hymn 'Crown Him With Many Crowns', setting a majestic tone for the programme. It was a powerful start to the programme, with so much life and energy. Senior leader Tony Morton then provided an insightful introduction to the church, emphasising its extensive work beyond Sunday services, including running Alpha courses, engaging in social action and involvement in international missions. He highlighted the church's mission to ensure every member felt their contribution was valuable and impactful.

Eileen Wallis, the widow of Arthur Wallis, shared a touching reflection on their long-held vision of a lively, energetic church filled with people of all ages. This vision, she stated, was now being realised in the dynamic community she witnessed today.

The worship band had been brought in from another church in Brighton, which did cause one or two challenges with the team already functioning at Central Hall, but the BBC were insistent that they preferred to work with people they already knew. Despite the ruffling of some feathers, the band, led by Dave Fellingham, did a great job.

The next segment of the programme saw the band lead the congregation in a spirited rendition of 'Battle Belongs', followed by a feature on The King's School with an interview with teacher Peter Phillips. He was able to communicate the heart and ethos of the school, founded by the church in 1982.

Piedad Prowting, a counsellor from the Firgrove Family Centre, was interviewed next, sharing about the centre's vital work offering hope and support to women facing crisis pregnancies.

The next song, 'All Heaven Declares', accompanied a montage of images from various church activities, including main meetings, small groups, children's programmes and city prayer walks. Interviews with church members Lindsey Lee, Chris McBride and me added personal testimonies to the narrative.

The worship band leader then performed 'In Every Circumstance', followed by a segment featuring church leader, Dave Adcock. Dave was shown travelling by train to Belgium, discussing the church's involvement with international communities.

A particularly memorable moment is the song 'Knowing You', which began with a small group of Christians singing in French in Belgium and transitioned seamlessly to the congregation at Central Hall, continuing in English. The visual of raised arms and heartfelt worship added to the emotional depth of the service.

Dave Fellingham provided an interview about the evolving nature of worship and the new music emerging from contemporary churches, which is transforming worship practices across many congregations.

Tony Morton returned to reinforce the church's commitment to rational and credible faith, emphasising the church's pursuit of living out their beliefs day by day. Eileen Wallis shared a visionary dream from the 1950s, now fulfilled, of a highway filled with joyous people of all ages, celebrating their faith.

The band led the congregation in a beautiful rendition of 'Reign in Me', followed by Tony Morton's concluding prayer. The final song, 'Let Your Living Water Flow', captured the congregation in deep, spirited worship, with many visibly moved and engaged.

Tony Morton then closed with a powerful message about the church's mission. He said:

> We want to create a context where we can live together to glorify God and to express in the community round about the teachings of Jesus, not as a protest, but as a positive, caring contribution to help people enjoy life and discover more of God for themselves.

According to the BBC, the programme received more feedback than any programme they had produced up until that point. We also received correspondence across the nation and even some from overseas. One church leader told us some years later that watching that programme saved his ministry and gave him hope for the future.

The prophetic

In 1997, we hosted our first prophetic conference, which became an annual event. These conferences, led by Graham Cooke, attracted church leaders and individuals involved in prophetic ministry. The inaugural conference featured prominent figures such as Marc Dupont and John Paul Jackson, both of whom had significant roles in the Christian prophetic movement of the 1990s.

There had always been a strong emphasis and focus for the church on the prophetic and on spiritual gifts, but this period with Graham's involvement did raise the bar for us in regard to the prophetic. It also aligned us more closely with the growing prophetic movement.

This movement emphasised the resurgence and normalisation of prophetic gifts within the church, focusing on prophecy, dreams, visions and supernatural insights. It was closely linked with various revival and renewal movements, emphasising spiritual renewal, repentance and deeper experiences of God's presence. The prophetic movement shaped many believers, passionate about hearing God's voice and witnessing his power in their lives and communities.

Expectation

There was a growing expectation during the late 1990s that we were on course for a great revival that the early pioneers of our movement had anticipated. We had seen significant growth not just in terms of numerical growth but in depth and breadth of ministry. The impact of the Toronto Blessing had been significant, not just for us but for many churches in our city and nation.

Tony's clearly recognised apostolic ministry supporting church leaders and networks was growing; Graham Cooke's international prophetic ministry and training programmes were helping equip many leaders and churches in the prophetic; Steve Lee had formed the Miracle Street evangelistic ministry and was serving churches across the UK; Peter Butt had begun delivering high-quality theological and leadership training for leaders in developing nations; Lynn Swart was developing worship leaders, hosting conferences and supporting leaders in many places; for myself, the work with young people was opening up opportunities for collaboration with other like-minded groups in my nation and overseas.

We were witnessing the Ephesians ministries functioning interdependently in lots of different areas, yet all having a common home base, The Community Church, from which everyone was operating. We were seeking to model what an apostolic community or resource church should or could look like.

It wasn't without its tensions. There was always a challenge between the focus on the local and the focus on the broader national and international aspects of the ministry. Having the same leader leading both strands of the church's ministry added a level of complexity, but we were strong relationally and were able to work through any tensions that emerged.

There were tensions and there were also challenges. Our dear friend and faithful encourager, Eileen Wallis, passed away in 1997 and Tony Morton was diagnosed with non-Hodgkin lymphoma, a type of cancer that affects the lymphatic system that same year. Just over eighteen months later, Tony's wife, Hannah, was diagnosed with the same cancer. Thankfully, both Tony and Hannah fully recovered from the disease after extensive courses of chemotherapy, and they remain cancer free.

Flying High

In 1997 we had hosted our first Flying High international leaders' conference for church leaders from the Cornerstone churches in the UK and for overseas partners. This was to become an annual fixture in our church calendar. For four days in October, we gathered around 200 leaders for inspirational worship, prophetic teaching, workshops and seminars with plenty of space for fellowship and food. Many of the international partners were housed with church members and those in our church who were able, got involved with stewarding and catering of the conference.

Graham Cooke had already developed a loose affiliation of churches under the umbrella of UCM, or United Christian Ministries. He had suggested to these churches that UCM merge with Cornerstone, which was well received, and so a new name was agreed upon under which the churches would operate. That name was c.net, an appropriate and relevant name for the 1990s tech-era!

We approached the end of the second millennium with gratitude to God for the way he had led us and with great hope and expectation for what he was about to do.

Chapter Fifteen

A New Shape Emerges

As the 1990s ended, a new shape to our shared life and worship expression had emerged. At the start of the decade, we were a single congregation meeting in the Boldrewood lecture theatre, supported by home groups scattered across the city. But we had now blossomed into something more dynamic and diverse.

Gathering

We were now growing more comfortable in our new permanent home – Central Hall. This move had marked a significant chapter in our journey, yet our unwavering dedication to small groups and localised mission continued. Transitioning to the cell church model, we ensured that intimate community connections remained at the heart of our mission, while our commitment to serving our local communities through various projects stayed strong.

Our primary gathering remained at 10.00 a.m. every Sunday morning, a time that had become a weekly anchor for our congregation. We had ventured into new territory for a while, experimenting with dual services at 9.30 a.m. and 11.00 a.m., but found that splitting the community in this way didn't foster unity in the way we had hoped for. It also stretched our resources. Another attempt, a more laid-back breakfast gathering aimed at families – cheerfully dubbed TGI Sundays – also had a short run before we returned to our traditional format.

However, not all innovations faded. Sunday evenings had begun to buzz with a different energy, as the Evening Congregation, born out of the 'refreshing meetings' initiated in 1994, continued to flourish. This gathering became a beacon for young adults, drawing them in with its more informal atmosphere. It was a place for much greater creativity and experimentation. For example, we hosted regular 'alternative worship evenings', creatively driven gatherings that pushed the boundaries on traditional forms of worship. In contrast to standard worship meetings, these gatherings incorporated a mix of modern music, visual arts, reflective practices and interactive elements, creating an atmosphere that encouraged personal exploration and communal engagement. The ambiance was typically more relaxed and informal, allowing participants to connect with their spirituality in fresh and meaningful ways. We also hosted 'bite nights' where members of the congregation could explore relevant and topical subjects together with various contributions from a wide range of members.

A New Shape Emerges

A great sense of community began to emerge among this evening group and over time, a new leadership team emerged, spearheaded by Theo and Sarah Amer. Their influence and roles would be significant in shaping the future of our church.

Meanwhile, the youth congregation, Sublime, remained a key part of our ministry. Every Saturday evening, the Small Hall at Central Hall echoed with the sounds of laughter, learning and worship, as Dave Boniface, along with Andy Wright, Ben Hinks and a team of enthusiastic volunteers, guided this spirited group of young people in their faith journey.

The monthly outreach event designed for seniors in our community, known as Sunday Afternoon at Central Hall, had touched many lives. The leadership of the event had passed to John and Jean Fleming and Mervyn and Claire Suffield following the untimely passing of its beloved organiser, Colin Henderson, in 1999.

Another significant moment in our church's development was the return of the Eastleigh group, who had been planted out as a separate church in the 1980s, for a period. Rejoining us at Central Hall, they brought with them a depth of experience and devotion. Under the capable leadership of Allan and Liz Cox, this group were strengthened and were realigned with the church's vision and values. In time, they would be replanted back into Eastleigh and become known as our Northern Congregation, adding yet another vibrant layer to our ever-growing community.

The Flowers

And then there was The Flowers gathering on a Sunday afternoon on what is affectionately known as the Flowers Estate.

The Flowers Estate in Swaythling is a residential area with a rich history and distinctive character. Located in the northern part of the city, this estate was developed primarily in the 1920s and 1930s, during a period of significant suburban expansion in Southampton. It is named the Flowers Estate because many of the streets are named after flowers, such as Daisy Road, Honeysuckle Road and Violet Road, lending a unique and charming identity to the neighbourhood.

The estate was originally built as council housing to accommodate the growing working-class population of Southampton. The homes were designed in a traditional style, reflecting the architectural trends of the early twentieth century, with many featuring gardens and green spaces that enhanced the estate's appeal as a family friendly environment.

Over the years, the Flowers Estate has become a well-established community with a mix of privately owned and rented homes. The area is known for its close-knit community feel, with local amenities such as parks, schools and shops contributing to the quality of life for residents.

However, as economic conditions, housing policies and social dynamics changed over the decades, some areas within the estate have faced challenges related to poverty and social deprivation. These shifts have led to higher unemployment rates or employment in lower-paying jobs, contributing to financial hardship for some households. Areas facing economic deprivation often experience higher levels of crime, and the Flowers Estate was no exception. Issues such as anti-social behaviour, drug-related crime and property crime were becoming more prevalent, affecting residents' quality of life and sense of security.

Bob's story

Bob Light had moved to the city and joined the church in 1996. In 1997 he married Collette, and they were led by the Lord to move on to the Flowers Estate, the estate where Bob grew up.

Bob was born in Southampton in May 1951. In his early teens, despite having natural ability, he began to lose confidence in school and started hanging out with a friend who introduced him to smoking cannabis and sniffing solvents. Bit by bit, Bob lost sight of school and his future, and drugs became his whole life.

One Friday, Bob arrived to find his regular dealer had run out of his usual supply. Undeterred, Bob turned to another dealer who immediately befriended him and took him to the park to smoke cannabis. This was simply a ploy to introduce Bob to heroin. At first, Bob refused; however, the dealer persisted, and with just one shot, Bob was hooked. The heroin shut out his world – he felt that nothing could touch him now. Sinking deeper into the drug culture, Bob was soon being supplied with drugs directly from his GP. At the age of seventeen, he was admitted to a psychiatric hospital for his first detoxification.

By the time of his first marriage at twenty-six, Bob had been sectioned into a psychiatric hospital five times for mental symptoms associated with drug use. His new wife was also a drug addict, and they would go together to get methadone prescriptions from their GP. In time, Bob became a big-time dealer. He went to Chinatown in London, contacted one of the city's drug barons, and soon became the biggest supplier of heroin in Southampton.

He eventually moved to Cornwall and took a job as a farmhand, but it was clear that Bob was still addicted to drugs, and his marriage fell apart. Thrown out of his family home, Bob became increasingly mentally unstable and was treated by the local psychiatrist. Rather than encouraging him to get clean, he was told to accept that he would always be a drug addict. Even though, deep down, Bob wanted to change, the input he was receiving led him to believe it would be impossible.

Sinking further into despair and depression, Bob persuaded a chemist to give him a three-day supply of drugs, claiming he was going to Scotland and wouldn't be able to come in for his daily collection. He drove himself onto the moors and injected the three-day supply all at once, hoping not to wake up. A knock on the car window the following morning made him jump. He wound down the window and was confronted by a man asking if he was alright. In the darkness, Bob hadn't noticed he had pulled into a layby outside a cottage, and the man at the window took him in. The man was an evangelist in the local church and offered Bob accommodation in his caravan across the road. As Bob was still living rough, he was pleased to accept.

Each day, the evangelist would spend an hour with Bob, talking to him about Jesus and taking him along to church on Sundays. The people of the local church did not recoil from Bob; they would come and give him a hug or put their arm around him. Bob was moved by their kindness, and longing to get free from his drug habits, he asked Jesus to change his life. The church prayed for him, and during a two-hour prayer meeting, Bob felt God's miraculous touch and was freed from drugs. He threw away all the drugs and needles he had in his pockets, and since that time, Bob has never taken drugs of any kind.

When the psychiatrist found out Bob was no longer taking drugs, he rang him, urging him to take a supply from the chemist, convinced that stopping suddenly would cause great harm. But Bob testified to God's goodness and declined the offer.

In 1996, Bob returned to Southampton and moved in with his mother on the Flowers Estate. Wanting to find a church, he opened the Yellow Pages and was drawn to an advert for The Community Church. He attended the next Sunday and knew immediately it was where God wanted him to be.

I remember a Sunday meeting in early 1997 at the end of the prophetic conference that we had hosted when Marc Dupont, one of the main speakers at the conference, picked Bob out and prophesied over him that he would be like 'a pied piper leading many people to Christ'.

This was one of several confirmations to Bob that he should move back onto the estate with his new wife, Collette, who had also recently become a Christian.

Back to the estate

They joined a local cell group led by a young couple in the church, Fred and Trish Gardiner. Bob and Collette encouraged the group to join them in prayer-walking the area. After a few months they began to connect with some of the disenfranchised young people on the streets, recognising that one of their reasons for struggles was simply that they had nothing to do. Bob and Collette and the group decided to start a youth club at the local Methodist church in Swaythling which they called Club Zion.

They were soon attracting a lot of young people and began to build relationships with their families. They discovered plenty of need in the community and simply began to address that need as they were able. Tidying gardens, accompanying people to court, helping those who were illiterate fill out forms, distributing food parcels, advising those in debt and supporting families in crisis were just some of the practical expressions of love that Bob and Collette began.

In the summer they organised a community weekend on Daisy Dip, a large green space in the middle of the estate, providing fun for the whole family with barbecues, music, games, inflatables and friendship. Bob's story and commitment to the gospel meant that over time several people from the estate made commitments to Christ. And because of the proximity of the estate to the university, quite a few students began to get involved with the work.

The distance from the estate to Central Hall and the lack of suitable transport for many people on the estate made attending Sunday meetings impractical. The solution was to start a gathering on a Sunday afternoon in the area. After much negotiation with Swaythling Methodist Church, there was an agreement to use the church hall for a regular meeting, simply called The Flowers.

The Flowers was a church for the unchurched. It held all the elements of a church service, but with a distinct flavour of its own, if not a little chaotic at times. As people arrived, they were greeted by the comforting aroma of toast, a simple yet warm offering that set the tone for the gathering. The scene was one of casual and organic community: families trickled in slowly, children in pushchairs, and young people pedalling up on their bikes, adding to the lively yet relaxed atmosphere.

Worship was generally led by a group of eager students, their guitars strumming in hopeful harmony. At that very first meeting, though the congregation's voices were few, their effort was sincere, a valiant attempt to raise praise in a space that felt more like a living room than a sanctuary. Children zoomed around the room on their small pushbikes, filling the air with the sound of wheels on wooden flooring.

When Bob stood up to speak, the room quieted with anticipation. He had such respect with those gathered. Week after week, he shared stories of Jesus with a passion that resonated deeply, his words planting seeds of faith in fertile hearts. The impact was profound. Over time, people were not just attending; they were being discipled, growing in their faith with each passing Sunday. The ripples of this transformation were visible and over the next few years, scores of people chose to be baptised, marking the start of their new journeys.

The commitment to this community extended beyond the Sunday gatherings. Several students and members of the church moved from the Central Hall congregation on to the estate, their presence a deliberate act of service to further the mission. The annual Dip Week became a highlight of the year, with regular teams of young people from Operation Mobilisation coming from all over the world to support the flourishing ministry.

To sustain and expand their efforts, Flowers of Justice was established as a charity. It became a beacon of hope, offering debt counselling, food distribution and family support to those in need. The church was no longer confined to walls and services; it became an active, living expression of justice and compassion.

Bob was not just a pastor to the attendees of the Flowers Church, which by now gathered every Sunday afternoon. He was a shepherd to the entire estate, a familiar and comforting presence during both celebrations and sorrows. Over the years, he conducted countless weddings and funerals, made multiple trips to court with those from the estate, visited many in prison, supported those coming off drugs and so much more, his influence weaving the community together like threads in a rich tapestry.

This has to be one of the highlights of our church's ministry from the past fifty years.

Chapter Sixteen

All Together Now

One of the earliest dreams and aspirations of the pioneers of the Restoration movement, along with the newly emerging church leaders, was the dismantling of denominational barriers and the creation of a much more visible expression of church unity. The baptism in the Holy Spirit had served as a powerful and unifying experience, drawing people together from across a broad Christian denominational spectrum. It was the fervent hope of these early trailblazers that this profound experience would continue to foster greater collaboration and unity among believers. These pioneers were convinced that God was actively working to unite his body, encouraging cooperation and fellowship across historic denominational lines, and acknowledging the universal body of Christ as a whole.

Opposition

However, in the 1970s and 1980s in Southampton, this vision of unity was not yet fully realised. As our new church grew during those early years, many Christians from other established churches in the city and surrounding region left their existing congregations to join what was then known as Southampton Christian Fellowship, which later evolved into Southampton Community Church.

For the ministers and leaders of these traditional churches, this created a significant degree of suspicion, with many accusing us of 'sheep stealing' – a term used to describe the practice of luring members away from other congregations. Consequently, these leaders tended to keep their distance from us. Additionally, there were others within the more conservative evangelical community who vehemently rejected the necessity of an additional experience of the Holy Spirit. On theological grounds, they were also unwilling to engage with us, perceiving our beliefs as a deviation from traditional evangelical doctrine.

One of the key figures opposing this movement was Dr Leith Samuel, the minister of Above Bar Church, who served the church from 1953 to 1980. The story of Dr Samuel is particularly intriguing, as he was a long-time family friend of Arthur Wallis, a prominent figure in the Restoration movement and key supporter of the Southampton Community Church. In fact, Arthur's father, Captain Reginald Wallis, had asked Leith in the 1930s to be a mentor to his two sons, Arthur and Peter, who were teenagers at the time. Leith accepted this responsibility with great seriousness, especially after the untimely death of Reginald just before the outbreak of the Second World War in 1939.

Leith played a pivotal role in Arthur's spiritual journey, arranging for his baptism at a hastily organised special service in the spring of 1942 before Arthur was posted overseas with the British Army. Throughout Arthur's deployment in North Africa as part of the Royal Tank Regiment in 1943, Leith maintained a steady stream of correspondence, sending long letters filled with spiritual encouragement and news from back home. These letters were a lifeline for Arthur, providing him with spiritual sustenance and a sense of connection to his faith during the trials of war. Arthur, in turn, wrote back as often as possible, sharing his experiences and the lessons God was teaching him in the midst of the conflict.

After the war, Arthur spent some time at the home of Leith and his wife, Mollie. It was during this period that Arthur met a close friend of Mollie's, Eileen Hemingway, who would later become his wife.

Despite their deep personal connection, theological differences between Leith and Arthur eventually led to some difficult conversations. Leith, a staunch advocate of Free Church and reformed Baptist principles, was vocally opposed to the baptism of the Holy Spirit, which placed him at odds with the emerging charismatic and Restoration movements that Arthur had become involved in. Nevertheless, despite their differing theological views, Arthur and Leith, along with Eileen and Mollie, managed to maintain their friendship for many years.

Shift

However, a significant shift began to occur in the 1990s in the city. Several factors contributed to this change, including the departure of leaders who had opposed the church, the arrival of new leaders in the city who were more open to churches like ours, and the recognition that after almost twenty years, we were here to stay and had proven to be theologically 'sound'. Additionally, several other churches in the city had also experienced the baptism of the Holy Spirit and had connected with national networks, further bridging the gap between us.

Up until this point, the main ecumenical body in the city was the Southampton Evangelical Alliance. We had been represented on this body for quite some time, with one of our leaders, Allan Cox, even serving as chair for a while. Allan did an outstanding job in allaying people's fears about our church, our theology and our motives. The Alliance was a broad group, drawing members from a wide range of denominational backgrounds – Anglican, Baptist, Free Evangelical, traditional Pentecostal and an increasing number of new churches.

In the mid to late 1990s, a new group began to emerge within the city, comprised of leaders who had all embraced the fresh work of the Holy Spirit, which became known as the Toronto Blessing (mentioned earlier). This new wave of Holy Spirit activity had a profound influence on churches across a wide spectrum of denominations, particularly those that had already embraced the charismatic renewal of the 1960s and 1970s, as well as churches impacted by the ministry of John Wimber. These churches – mainly Anglican, Methodist and Baptist – were now attending festivals such as New Wine, Spring Harvest and Soul Survivor, where they were not only exposed to teaching about the work of the Holy Spirit but were also experiencing fresh, transformative encounters with the

Spirit. This common experience, rather than a shared creed or doctrinal position, became the starting point for a much greater sense of unity among the churches.

This emerging group, which came to be known as Streams in the City, recognised we were all part of the same 'river' but each 'stream' flowed distinctively into that one river, included leaders from The King's Church, part of the Ichthus network, City Gate Church, members of the Pioneer network, an Elim Pentecostal church, two Assemblies of God churches, a couple of Anglican churches and the Southampton Vineyard church. We began to meet frequently for prayer and fellowship, and as a result, relationships deepened, mutual trust was established and we began to explore what we could do together to serve and impact our city for the gospel.

One of the first significant initiatives supported by the Streams in the City group was The Dell '98 youth event, which demonstrated the potential of collective action. The success of this event made it clear that our combined energy and resources could be a powerful force for good in Southampton.

Momentum

Building on this momentum, a proposal was developed to host an outdoor joint service on Pentecost Sunday, 11th June 2000. The Streams in the City group would take on the responsibility of organising the event, and we all agreed to close our Sunday morning services that day, to gather at Mayflower Park, located next to the Southampton waterfront. In a bold move, we also decided to invite other church leaders to join us for the celebration, including Father John O'Shea, priest in charge of St Edmund's Roman Catholic Church, and Dr John Balchin, the interim leader of Above Bar Church, the large Free Evangelical Church in the city centre. This was significant for a couple of reasons. Firstly, the leadership of Above Bar Church had initially taken a strong stance against the charismatic renewal, and secondly, constitutionally, Above Bar Church leaders were not allowed to share a platform with Roman Catholics. But they agreed to join us!

Having both leaders from very different denominational backgrounds share a platform on the day we celebrated the birth of the Church of Jesus Christ on Pentecost Sunday was a momentous occasion.

After many months of careful planning and negotiation with the City Council, the day finally arrived. We were blessed with fine weather on that Sunday as church members from across the city made their way down to the waterfront. There was ample parking in Mayflower Park and the surrounding area. A large stage had been set up, and the worship band, composed of members from several different churches, was ready to lead us. By the time Tony Morton welcomed everyone to this special occasion, nearly 1,500 people had gathered in the congregation. Some were seated on the grass, others had spread out blankets on the ground, some were in camping chairs, while others stood around the edges, eager to participate in this historic event. The worship was heartfelt and moving, and there were contributions from several church leaders, including the aforementioned Father John O'Shea and Dr John Balchin, who offered words of encouragement and prayers for unity and renewal.

After the formal service, people lingered in the park with their picnics, while children played in the nearby playground. There was a palpable sense of joy and community as people slowly packed up and made their way home, knowing that they had been part of something truly special.

Collaboration

This event provided the platform and catalyst for a new season of much greater collaboration among churches in the city. The Streams in the City group eventually evolved into the Joshua Partnership, which began meeting weekly for prayer and fellowship. For three consecutive years, from 2001 to 2003, we organised the Hi-Life Festival, a two-week-long event that enabled all churches to engage in local outreach, with a few key events hosted centrally.

One year, we hosted the innovative On the Move BBQ in the city centre with London-based evangelist Martin Graham. This free barbecue provided an opportunity for church members to engage in conversations about Jesus with those enjoying the burgers and hot dogs. Another year, we hosted a series of comedy nights featuring a range of Christian comedians, and in the final year, we hired Southampton Guildhall for a series of evangelistic events with Robert Maasbach, an evangelist from the Netherlands, who shared a powerful testimony of God's healing and salvation.

Annual Pentecost prayer and worship gatherings at Central Hall also became a regular feature during this time, further strengthening the bonds between the churches.

In 2005, the Southampton Evangelical Alliance, chaired by Graham Archer, vicar of Highfield Church of England, merged with the Joshua Partnership to form the Southampton Christian Network (SCN).

Graham and his family had recently arrived in the city. As a member of the New Wine network and a supporter of the charismatic renewal movement, he brought significant energy to his role as vicar. He quickly became involved in broader city activities and established strong relationships with members of the Joshua Partnership. Eager to foster unity, Graham took on the responsibility of chairing the newly formed SCN, supported by a small coordinating team from various churches.

The SCN's stated vision was:

> To be a network of Christian churches and organisations working together towards the salvation and transformation of Southampton and the surrounding area. The SCN would provide a forum for evangelical church and organisation leaders to connect and collaborate. It would offer opportunities for mutual support, prayer, and worship. The SCN would also serve as a communication network for sharing ideas and initiatives within member organizations and beyond. Additionally, the SCN would act as a corporate voice to the city council, media, police, and other key groups in the city. The SCN would work in partnership with the broader Christian community in Southampton, such as Churches Together in Southampton, on issues affecting all of us.

The steering team did extensive work in defining its values, leading to the following commitments:

> We recognise that the gospel is rooted in relationships, and we aim to promote good and faithful relationships between Christian leaders, churches, organisations, and the entire church community in our shared relationship with God.
>
> We will endeavour to work collaboratively in our mission to the city, recognizing when collective efforts are more effective than individual ones.
>
> We will share good practices and expertise to resource one another's initiatives.
>
> We will seek God together in prayer as we strive to fulfil the Great Commission.
>
> We will establish structures for fellowship among Christian leaders as needed.
>
> We will communicate clearly and effectively about the challenges and opportunities that God presents in the city.
>
> We will respond corporately to issues that impact our mission.

This marked a significant step forward in the unity and collaboration among churches in the city.

Growing unity

A short time later, Above Bar Church appointed a new minister, John Risbridger. This was John's first church leadership role, having previously been head of Student Ministries at the Universities and Colleges Christian Fellowship (UCCF). John's wife, Alison, was from a family who had a long history with the charismatic renewal. And so, we had in John another significant leader in the city who was sympathetic to things of the Spirit and with a heart for church unity.

This growing unity in the period from the late 1990s to the mid-2000s, leading up to the formation of the SCN, was a key factor in the significant impact the church was having in many areas of the city.

Between September 2003 and March 2005, the Southampton City Mission and the Shaftesbury Society conducted and collated research into church-led activities serving people in the city. In early 2006, the Saints of a Different League report was published. The report highlighted:

> . . . the important contribution that the church makes in addressing needs in the city. The history and breadth of the projects is remarkable as is the level of dedication by paid staff and volunteers.

The report identified 126 different community projects staffed by 106 full-time members of staff and fifty-three part-time members. These projects were served by 1,365 volunteers and a total of 6,909 'users' benefited from these various community projects. The report went on to state:

Many individuals see their involvement in these activities as an integral outworking of their faith, following Jesus' commandment 'to love their neighbour as themselves' [Matthew 22:37-39]. This is having a positive impact on the quality of life of thousands of people every week.

The church is fulfilling a vital role in bringing people together and building community, whether in a particular geographical area of the city or within particular groups of people. These activities are helping to alleviate the increasing isolation and loneliness so common in our individualistic society. The church is also providing a huge number of activities for children; safe places where they can have fun and learn life skills.

Several projects have been running for decades, long before and after many government initiatives have been set up. Many have a proven long-term commitment to an area or client group in the city which can often go unnoticed by the wider church and other agencies.

There is still much to be done but there is a great basis of experience, dedication, creativity, energy and compassion upon which to build.[8]

As we pursued God's mission in our city together, we were deeply aware of how far we had come, and we gave thanks for the opportunities to work alongside so many different congregations to see lives transformed by the gospel. We remained committed to breaking down any barriers that existed between the various churches, and continued to strive to fulfil the vision of a united Church, working together for the glory of God in Southampton and beyond.

In the end, it is God that creates the unity. There is no doubt that his work in each of us as leaders, and through the leaders to the congregations, produced a God-given unity that significantly affected our city. We are grateful to this day for that shared unity.

Chapter Seventeen

TRANSITION

As the dawn of the new millennium broke, our journey reached a significant milestone. What began in 1975 as a small, dedicated group of believers had blossomed into a vibrant and diverse congregation, now a prominent and influential pillar of Southampton's faith community.

Faith in action

By the time the new millennium arrived, we had become more than just a gathering of believers; we were a thriving community, united by faith and a shared commitment to making a difference in the world. The church's expansion was not only in numbers but also in the diversity of its mission. People from various walks of life had found a spiritual home within our walls, drawn together by a common purpose. This growth was a testament to our ability to adapt and thrive amid changing times, staying true to our core mission while embracing new opportunities.

The transition into the new millennium also marked a deepening of our commitment to community outreach and mission. Dave Adcock and the French group had recently acquired a large property with land just outside the town of Vire in Normandy. This new base, named Sans Frontières, was envisioned as a neutral space for French Christians to gather as well as a place of hospitality and prayer for those from outside France. Meanwhile, Steve Lee's Miracle Street evangelistic ministry was working with churches across the nation, and Peter Butt's School of Ministries was now rolling out theological and leadership training in various nations across Africa and Asia.

We recognised that our mission extended beyond spiritual nourishment to include tangible acts of service and compassion. This era saw us engage more actively in addressing local issues. John Deagle, a founding member and leader in the church, together with Paul and Janice Finn, leaders of a local Assemblies of God church, had established the Southampton Family Trust, offering vital support for marriages across the city. Additionally, a ten-bedroom property in the city was gifted to us on a long-term peppercorn rent, which we decided to use as a supported housing project named The Sanctuary, providing a safe space for eight to ten men recovering from addiction. These initiatives were powerful expressions of faith in action, making a meaningful impact on countless lives.

Learning

Leadership had been a constant force throughout our short history, with the same dedicated leadership couple guiding us since 1976, a year after our inception. Tony and Hannah Morton's vision and unwavering faith were instrumental in steering the church through periods of change and challenge, helping us grow in both strength and spirit. However, as the church entered the new millennium, it was also time for new leadership to emerge, bringing fresh perspectives and renewed energy to our mission.

Having been a part of the church since 1982 and on the staff team in various capacities since 1984, I now found myself as part of the main leadership team. My responsibilities included overseeing our work with the 'next generation', running our Year of Training discipleship programme alongside Phil Orchard, leading and speaking regularly at Central Hall, and being part of a strategy team with Tony, Graham Cooke and Adrian Thomas, responsible for the future development of the church.

We had grown to become a very diverse and complex organisation, and none of us had much training or experience in managing such an entity. I recall a meeting where Tony asked, 'I wonder what modern companies are learning about leadership and management that could help us?' He specifically mentioned companies like The Body Shop. We all nodded in agreement, and the meeting ended with a sense of curiosity about what we could learn.

The following Sunday, I was speaking at Arun Community Church, a place I regularly visited. After the service, I found myself in conversation with someone new. He introduced himself as Jim, from Scotland, and as we talked, I discovered that he worked for The Body Shop, which had its headquarters in Littlehampton, the hometown of Arun Community Church. Intrigued, I asked about his role. 'I'm the head of Leadership Development, responsible for leadership training across the business,' he replied. Taken aback by the coincidence, I told him about our recent discussion regarding leadership in organisations like The Body Shop. I invited Jim to come to Southampton to meet Tony, Graham and others on the team to explore how his insights might help us.

Jim soon became a valued friend and advisor, meeting regularly with myself, Caroline, Tony and Graham. The four of us even formed a small advisory group to Jim as he transitioned from his role at The Body Shop to take on a wider leadership consultancy role, supporting individuals, churches, charities and businesses.

Jim helped us understand how to lead amid complexity. He taught us that in any organisation, there are few things we can be certain about. We can have certainty about some areas, such as finances, health and safety, and safeguarding. These are very important and, in these areas, we create rules and policies to help us. However, much of our work involves navigating uncertainty because we are dealing with people, each with their own agendas, surprises that disrupt our daily lives and questions we simply cannot answer.

The key to thriving in what might appear a chaotic environment was to establish our core commitments and work diligently at maintaining strong relationships. This may seem simple, but it was incredibly valuable as we considered the implications of leadership transition.

Senior leader

In early 2001, Tony shared with me his decision to step down from the leadership of the church in Southampton so he could focus more fully on the growing work of c.net nationally and internationally. He asked what I thought about taking on the role of senior leader at The Community Church. I had been very focused on my work with young people and the next generation of leaders, and I was travelling and ministering in different settings outside of the church. I was more of a visionary leader and less of a pastoral leader than maybe was required for a local church leader. And I felt that there were others on the leadership team who might better fit the role of church leader.

But I knew that God had already spoken.

In late 1994, while at the Toronto Airport Christian Fellowship, I had a profound experience. Responding to a call during one of the meetings, I found myself 'slain in the Spirit', lying on my back. As I lay there on that grey carpet, I clearly heard the voice of the Lord say, 'I have called you to lead The Community Church, Southampton.' It was a complete shock, as this was the furthest thing from my mind at the time. Upon returning home, I chose not to share this with anyone, except for Caroline.

Fast forward seven years, and now I am having a conversation with Tony about taking on the role of senior leader. After years of feeling a deep, unwavering sense of calling, the invitation to become the leader of the church had arrived. I'd never shared my experience in Toronto or tried to manipulate anything, I had simply served as faithfully and diligently as I could in the areas that I had been given responsibility for. It was a surreal moment, one filled with both a profound sense of confirmation and overwhelming humility. I had always known in my heart that this was my destiny, that God had been preparing me for this role long before the offer was made. But now that moment had come, the weight of the responsibility felt more tangible than ever.

At the same time, I had a deep sense of peace that accompanies the call, as if God was reassuring me that he would provide the strength, vision and guidance I would need to fulfil the role. Stepping into the position felt like stepping into a promise – a promise I'd held onto for a long time, and now it was unfolding before me.

I discussed it with Caroline, our friend Jim, and a few other trusted friends outside the church. As we talked and reflected, it became clear that this was the right path. I knew I would need to re-evaluate my time and commitments to ensure I could fulfil the role effectively. However, I felt confident that with our strong relational values and the input we had received from Jim, we could navigate this transition successfully. Tony would remain part of the church, offering support and advice, allowing us to model a healthy transition.

Caroline and I met with Tony and Hannah, and together we decided on a course of action. We first communicated the decision to the leadership team, with Tony having already met with most of the team one-on-one to gather their feedback. We then shared the news with the wider leaders and trustees, and once all key stakeholders were informed, we announced the leadership transition to the whole church in the autumn of that year. The handover weekend was scheduled for Saturday, 19th and Sunday, 20th January of the following year, 2002.

Transition weekend

One of the invaluable lessons we learned from our friend Jim was the significance of acknowledging the emotions tied to any transition in life. Whether it's moving to a new home, changing jobs, or mourning the loss of a loved one, the emotions we experience follow a similar pattern. We often navigate through stages of fear, anxiety and despair before finding ourselves in a new place of hope and embracing possibilities for the future that lies ahead.

With this understanding, we invited Jim to facilitate a day dedicated to the transition of leadership on Saturday, 19th January, at Central Hall.

People began arriving steadily for the 10 a.m. start, their expressions a blend of nervousness and excitement. After a time of worship led by Lynn Swart, Jim kicked off the day with a session focused on the process of change. He spoke about the sense of loss we encounter, the emotions that accompany it, and the hope that eventually emerges as we journey through this process.

Tony then took the stage to share his personal journey. He reflected on how the church was formed, the challenges we've faced together, his aspirations for the future and his own plans for ministry.

Following Tony's talk and before lunch, Jim introduced an exercise he called The Change Model. This was a physical activity designed to help participants process change by moving from station to station around the room. Each station featured a sheet of paper with a thought-provoking question. These questions guided us through the stages of change, encouraging us to jot down our responses before moving on to the next station.

The questions ranged from, 'What was good about the way things were before the change?' to 'What could be the impact of the change on you?' to 'What's the worst that could happen?' and, 'What might you now need to do?' We also considered, 'What could this change facilitate for you?' and, 'What might now be possible?' These questions provided a space for everyone to explore and process the emotions connected to the change.

After lunch, Tony and I hosted a Q&A session. Members of the congregation asked a variety of questions about Tony's decision to step down, why he believed I was the right person to take on the role, how Tony would continue to be involved, what my plans were for the future of the role, and how Tony and I would collaborate in this new arrangement. The openness and transparency of the session made it a particularly healthy and constructive conversation.

I concluded the day by sharing more about my own journey, my calling, and how I envisioned the future unfolding.

That evening, we took time to unwind with a buffet meal prepared by some of the congregation members. For entertainment, we were treated to a performance by Christian comedian Milton Jones, known for his quirky, surreal one-liners and trademark wild hair. A regular on BBC Radio 4 and popular UK panel shows like *Mock the Week*, Milton's unique comedic style was a hit. He humorously introduced himself as 'Billy's assistant leader', adding a delightful touch to the evening.

Generations, Generations, Generations

The following day, Sunday morning, Central Hall was packed. I looked around a little nervously as the seats filled. Here were my friends, those I had journeyed with, those who had discipled me as much as me discipling them. I felt God's assurance, his comfort, stilling my nerves.

The Sunday Morning Congregation was joined by members from the Northern Congregation in Eastleigh, the Evening Congregation, the Sublime Congregation, and people from the Flowers Estate.

The meeting began at 10.00 a.m., buzzing with anticipation. Dave Adcock and Allan Cox hosted, warmly welcoming everyone and outlining the schedule for this special Sunday morning. Lynn Swart, accompanied by the band, led the congregation in exuberant and heartfelt worship. As usual, the children left at 10.40 a.m. for their respective activities. Then, much like the previous day, Tony and I had the opportunity to share insights about the journey so far and our hopes for the future.

The event then moved into the commissioning. Caroline and I sat at the front as Tony, Hannah and Graham gathered around us. Tony delivered a strong prophetic word, saying, 'When I was appointed to leadership, the word spoken over me was "nations, nations, nations", but the word I speak over you is "generations, generations, generations", signifying the focus of your ministry.' Hannah then presented Caroline with an ornate antique key, saying, 'This key symbolises authority, and today, God gives it to you. It will open every door in this house, granting you the right to enter every room.' The other leaders then gathered around us, laid hands on us, and prayed as we embarked on this new journey.

It was a powerful and deeply moving moment. And we realised that, for us, the real work now began.

Chapter Eighteen

The First Year

Organisations and movements typically experience significant changes over a thirty-year cycle, a pattern often observed across religious, political and social groups. This cycle generally progresses through stages of inception, growth, maturity and sometimes decline or reinvention.

Decades

In the initial decade, organisations are marked by rapid growth and innovation, driven by the founding members' clear vision and purpose. This period is characterised by a high level of energy, creativity, and a willingness to experiment and take risks. The focus is on establishing a strong foundation, developing core values and attracting like-minded individuals who share the vision.

As organisations enter their second decade, they begin a phase of consolidation and formalisation. The initial enthusiasm gives way to the creation of structures, policies and traditions that provide stability and continuity. Growth continues, but it becomes more measured and strategic, with a greater emphasis on long-term planning. Leadership transitions may start to occur, potentially bringing new perspectives but also the challenge of maintaining the original vision.

By the third decade, challenges may emerge. Organisations may face stagnation, an identity crisis, or external pressures that force them to reassess their direction. The original vision may become diluted or lose relevance as the context in which the organisation operates changes. This can lead to internal conflicts or a push for reinvention. Organisations that successfully navigate this phase can experience revitalisation, while those that fail to adapt may decline.

Thirty-year cycle

As our church approached the end of this thirty-year cycle, it became evident that the move to Central Hall and the fresh influence of the Holy Spirit in the mid-90s had likely extended our vitality into this third phase. We had managed to transition leadership while maintaining continuity with the existing team, and welcomed fresh leadership, such as Theo and Sarah Amer, in their mid-twenties, who had been leading the Sunday Evening Congregation. Theo's appointment to a full-time role on the leadership team as my executive assistant exemplified this blend of continuity and new energy.

New leaders continued to emerge within various settings, ensuring a steady flow of fresh ideas and perspectives. Ben Hinks, in his early twenties, stepped into a leadership role in the Sublime youth congregation, bringing a renewed sense of purpose and direction. Recent graduates Tom Waterton and Rachel Edwards took over the responsibility of the student work, ensuring that the younger generation remained engaged and connected to the church. Meanwhile, Clive Wiseman succeeded John Duff as chair of trustees, overseeing the governance and financial stewardship.

This combination of experienced leadership and new voices allowed for sustained growth and development during the first eighteen months to two years after the leadership transition. To help us navigate this season we formed a new group to assist us that we called our Oversight Group. This group drew together the trustees, the leadership team and some who had previously been in leadership as well as several long-standing and respected church members. This group of about forty also became the members of our charitable company.

Reporting change

If you have ever travelled, you'll be aware of the help that photos provide after the event. What might otherwise be recalled in a muddled way can be accurately recollected by way of a picture. As a church and, increasingly, a movement, we were on the cusp of more significant changes. So, to have a snapshot of church at a specific moment is very helpful. The church's Annual Report for 2003 provides such a snapshot – an overview of the progress made up to August 2003. It highlights the various ministries and congregations that contributed to the church's overall health and vitality.

Central Hall – Sunday Morning

The Central Hall Sunday Morning Congregation continued to flourish, with approximately 600 members gathering each week for worship. The services were designed to cater to a diverse congregation, incorporating different worship styles and teaching content that resonated with various ages and social backgrounds. The introduction of a new video projection system significantly enhanced the worship experience, allowing for more dynamic and engaging services. This congregation, being the largest, served as a hub for the church's broader activities, embodying the church's commitment to inclusivity and community.

Central Hall – Sunday Evening

In contrast to the morning service, the Sunday Evening Congregation offered a more intimate worship experience. Typically attended by seventy to 100 people, most of whom were aged eighteen to thirty, this service provided a space for deeper reflection and more personal connections. The relaxed atmosphere, combined with the use of modern technology such as lights and visual effects, created a unique worship environment that resonated with younger adults and those seeking a more contemplative approach.

Northern Congregation

The Northern Congregation, located in Eastleigh, experienced significant growth and change, with its membership increasing to around 250 people. One of the most notable aspects of this congregation was *Kidz Club*, an outreach initiative aimed at unchurched children in the local community. With over thirty dedicated helpers, *Kidz Club* played a crucial role in engaging with families who might not otherwise have had contact with the church.

Sublime Youth Congregation

Sublime Youth Congregation thrived under the leadership of Ben Hinks and his team. 'The Gathering', the main youth service, consistently attracted around 150 teenagers, creating a vibrant and energetic environment for worship and fellowship. The congregation also organised 'Big Story' events, which drew approximately 500 young people from diverse backgrounds, providing an opportunity for outreach and evangelism. Leadership development remained a key priority, with multiple training groups running alongside ten cell groups, a worship development group and a dance training group. The youth also engaged in mission work, with twenty-one members participating in trips to the USA and Germany, broadening their understanding of global ministry and service.

The Flowers Congregation

The work on the Flowers Estate continued to make significant progress. The Sunday afternoon children's club, *Club Zion*, remained the focal point of the congregation's outreach efforts. A new visitation programme was introduced, involving weekly home visits to the families of children attending the club. This initiative helped to build stronger relationships within the community and provided a more holistic approach to ministry. Teenage cell groups continued to meet weekly, offering a safe space for young people to explore their faith. The summer event, *Dip Week*, was particularly successful, strengthening community ties and providing a platform for further outreach.

Pastoral developments

The Central Pastoral Team expanded to over thirty members, reflecting the church's commitment to providing comprehensive care and support to its members. The shift from a geographically based system of care to a more congregational approach allowed for greater flexibility in addressing the diverse needs of the church community. This approach also ensured that deep friendships and small group connections remained intact, even as the church continued to grow. Marriage preparation courses were expanded, recognising the importance of strong, healthy marriages in the life of the church. The *Get Real* programme continued to have a profound impact, offering practical and spiritual guidance to those facing life's challenges.

Harvesters

Harvesters, a ministry founded fifteen years ago to support the needs of more mature church members, continued its work with great success. The ministry's popular walks and annual weekend away provided opportunities for fellowship and spiritual growth, attracting members from other local churches as well. *Harvesters* played a crucial role in ensuring that older members of the congregation remained active and engaged in the life of the church, contributing their wisdom and experience to the broader community.

Deeper in the Word

The *Deeper in the Word* programme, designed to provide in-depth Bible teaching, saw significant growth. Serving over thirty students, the programme offered twelve modules from the *School of Ministries*, covering a wide range of theological topics. This programme not only deepened the biblical knowledge of participants but also equipped them for various forms of ministry within the church and beyond.

Alpha Course

The *Alpha course* remained a cornerstone of the church's outreach efforts, providing a welcoming environment for those exploring the Christian faith. The course continued to bring many to faith, offering a strong foundation in the basics of Christianity. This year's highlight was the Alpha Regional Day at Central Hall, which attracted around 200 attendees. The event served as a powerful reminder of the course's impact, not just within the church, but across the region.

Central Counselling and Training Service

The Central Counselling and Training Service had a particularly productive year. With a team of around thirty-five, the service provided essential support to the congregation and the wider community. Over eighty individuals received counselling, and 100 students completed courses in various aspects of counselling and pastoral care. The service also strengthened its partnerships with other churches and counselling centres, expanding its reach and impact.

The Sanctuary

A significant development was the offer of a ten-year lease for a property to serve as a supported housing facility. This property, known as The Sanctuary, could accommodate up to eight people transitioning from an addictive lifestyle. Ross Hoare was appointed as the centre manager, bringing his experience and passion for helping others to this new initiative. The Sanctuary represented a major step forward in the church's mission to support those in recovery, providing a safe and nurturing environment for individuals to rebuild their lives.

The King's Primary School

The King's Primary School had a good year, achieving excellent SATs results and expanding its provision for children with special needs. The school's strong sense of community was evident in the active participation of parents in school life. The school's success reflected its commitment to academic excellence and its dedication to nurturing the whole child, both academically and spiritually.

The Central Hall Community Gospel Choir

The Central Hall Community Gospel Choir continued to engage the local community through music. The choir performed at various events and workshops, bringing the joy and energy of gospel music to a wide audience. Members, regardless of their musical experience, contributed through hard work and enthusiasm, ensuring high-quality performances. The choir was not just a musical group, but a ministry in its own right, using the power of music to build bridges and bring people together.

Hi-Life Big Band

The Hi-Life Big Band, directed by Andrew Worsfold, gained significant momentum over the year. The band performed at large venues such as Central Hall and Southampton Guildhall, and participated in various events, including *Miracle Street* initiatives. The band's dynamic performances and wide repertoire made it a popular fixture at church and community events alike.

Miracle Street

Miracle Street, a major evangelistic initiative, saw the successful launch of The Bandwagon, a mobile 500-seat arena. The Bandwagon quickly became the centrepiece of major missions, bringing the gospel to a wide audience in various locations. Alongside The Bandwagon, The Truck, a mobile stage vehicle, was used to reach even more people with the message of hope. These innovative tools allowed the church to take its message beyond the walls of Central Hall, engaging with communities in new and creative ways.

Overseas Mission

The Mission Support Group remained highly active, producing a comprehensive Missions Policy Document that outlined the church's approach to international ministry. The church continued to support individuals serving abroad, with a particular focus on countries such as France, Kenya, India, Nepal and Spain. These international connections enriched the church's understanding of global Christianity and provided opportunities for cross-cultural exchange and learning.

c.net expansion

c.net experienced significant growth, developing both a Mission and Training team and a Church Care team. The expansion of prophetic ministry was a notable development, providing spiritual guidance and encouragement to both individuals and the church. The annual leaders' event, *Flying High*, was a major success, attracting 350 attendees and serving as a catalyst for further growth and development within the network. c.net's overseas care initiatives also saw considerable progress, with efforts in Kenya, India, Nepal and Spain leading to meaningful and lasting impact.

In addition to all the above and recognising the need for improved facilities, a Building Group was formed to plan a major refurbishment of Central Hall. There was a lot of infrastructure work now required including a complete rewire and significant heating upgrade. We also wanted to enhance the sense of welcome from the entrance area and into the Main Hall.

Plans were developed for the foyer, to provide full access for disabled people at the main entrance to the building and first floor, the creation of a reception area and new doors to comply with fire regulations. The most ambitious part of the plan was the redevelopment of the Main Hall with the removal of the limited barriers separating the upper and lower seating areas, together with the provision of new and up-to-date seating, and the raising of the floor, which in turn made the staging area more accessible. In addition, there was a complete redecoration transforming the appearance of the hall without losing the character and feel of this majestic facility.

Plans were agreed and the budget was set. Our task was to raise just over £1 million. Written on a page like this, it seems almost reasonable. But it was a huge step of faith for us at the time and an almost impossible task without God's help.

Chapter Nineteen

DOUBLE WHAMMY!

The year 2004 began on a promising note.

We secured the use of a community facility on the Flowers Estate, owned by the City Council, which provided us with a base for our work on the estate and for our Sunday gatherings. Additionally, we were gifted a second residential property – a five-bedroom house in Midanbury – by a small charity that could no longer manage it. This house, bestowed as a permanent endowment, was to be used for housing and the relief of poverty for those in need. It had historically served as a sanctuary for missionaries on furlough, who stayed for three to six months. We eventually sold this property and purchased two smaller properties, which we were able to utilise effectively over the following years.

Gift Day

In May of that year, we launched an appeal for the refurbishment of Central Hall and held our first Gift Day, where we raised just over an astonishing £200,000 in a single offering from the congregation. This was a remarkable offering where we raised more than twice as much as the very first church offering for the purchase of Central Hall back in 1989.

However, not everything was without concern. The financial strain of managing The King's Primary School was becoming increasingly burdensome. Fewer families from the church were choosing to send their children to the school. Out of the 120 students, only twenty were from families attending The Community Church. Ken Ford had returned from Bridgwater, where he had been leading the church, and had taken on the role of headteacher. We began exploring options, including raising fees, closing the school, or merging once again with The King's School Senior.

The greatest challenge

Then, we faced the greatest challenge we had ever encountered.

It was Saturday, 5th June 2004 – a date forever etched in our family's memory, as it was the anniversary of the death of Caroline's brother, Graham. We had just returned from a family holiday in Canada, where we visited our eldest son, who was working as an intern at a large Christian activities centre north of Toronto.

We arrived home in Southampton that afternoon, and within minutes, the phone rang. On the other end was a rather subdued church leader, a close friend outside of our Southampton family. His voice was heavy as he spoke.

'Billy, I have some devastating news.'

My heart sank; I thought someone had died or there had been a tragic accident.

'I'm afraid I have to tell you that Tony had made some very poor decisions.'

I had to sit down. Tony? Tony Morton?

'You will need to call the leaders together and visit Tony and Hannah as soon as possible.'

It felt as if someone had punched me in the stomach.

I phoned Tony and informed him of the call. We arranged to visit that evening. When we arrived, we found Hannah distraught. Tony explained what had happened, holding nothing back. He was suggesting that, as far as he was concerned, their marriage had no future. We spent some time with them both, asking questions and trying to work out what the implications were. We left their home, deeply saddened.

I contacted each member of our leadership team, requesting they arrive at Central Hall an hour before the meeting the next morning.

That Sunday morning at 9.00 a.m. the leadership team gathered in our open-plan office behind the Main Hall stage. There was a palpable sense of unease and uncertainty. When everyone had arrived, I shared the news. The shock in the room was tangible; words were few. We had a meeting to conduct and had decided that nothing could be said until the situation became clearer.

Speed of change

On Monday, we convened with the church leadership and the broader c.net team. The atmosphere was sombre. We provided them with everything we knew and agreed to meet again before Friday to formulate a communication strategy as the situation evolved.

Then Thursday happened. On Thursday, 10th June, we received Tony's letter of resignation. It all happened so quickly – so shockingly fast.

On Friday, we met again as a leadership group to update everyone on the developments. We drafted a brief statement to be sent out to the churches, informing them that Tony had made some 'poor decisions' and had stepped down from his position, without providing further details.

The Community Church leadership team met again to plan how we would handle the gathering at Central Hall on Sunday. We knew we couldn't carry on as usual. We decided on a shortened meeting: a welcome, a song of worship, and then I would share the news. Dave Adcock, Allan Cox and Phil Orchard would lead prayers for Tony, Hannah, their family and the church. And with that, the meeting would end.

Sunday arrived faster than anyone anticipated, and an unsettling tension hung in the air. There was an unspoken understanding that something was amiss. Rumours had already begun to swirl. The usual full worship band was absent, replaced by a lone guitarist on stage, and the familiar buzz of anticipation that typically greeted the start of a meeting was conspicuously missing.

Our planned communication unfolded as well as could be expected, though it left many feeling deeply upset and troubled. Among those present were Michael and Amanda, attending the service for the first time. They would later become valued members of our congregation, citing the transparency and grace with which we, as leaders, handled the situation that Sunday as a significant factor in their decision to join the church.

...And following

The following weeks were incredibly challenging. We found ourselves in numerous meetings with various leaders and engaged in countless conversations with individuals. Tony decided to leave the family home, choosing instead to move to a house he and Hannah had purchased in Spain. From that point on, communication with Tony became increasingly infrequent.

In September, another blow struck us when Graham and Heather Cooke announced they were to separate. The circumstances were completely different, but Heather intended to relocate to Scotland, and Graham, understandably devastated, decided to relocate to the USA for an extended period and continue his ministry there.

This left us reeling. We had lost our main apostolic leader, and with Graham's move to the USA following the dissolution of his marriage, our primary prophetic leader as well. The personal devastation to their families was profound, but it also created a significant void in the leadership of both the church and the broader c.net ministry.

As part of Tony's repositioning after the leadership transition at The Community Church, the aim was to allow him to be more fully engaged with the development of the c.net ministry on both national and international levels. Graham also played a pivotal role alongside Tony in these efforts.

The pressing question we faced was: Who could step up to lead c.net? My role in leading the church was clear, and the leadership team was now well-established, providing a sense of continuity. The recently formed Church Oversight Group proved critical in helping us navigate local matters, but it was the broader leadership of the network that caused significant concern.

Consultations

The c.net team initiated a series of consultations with leaders from c.net churches across the UK to explore potential future leadership options for the network. International partners were kept in the communication loop and offered their input. However, over time it became evident that there was no one who could step up and assume the responsibility of leading the network. This led to the incredibly difficult decision to formally close the network.

Within c.net, clusters of churches had formed strong bonds, and these groups were encouraged to continue working together. Churches were also given the freedom to connect with other networks where they could find the support they needed. While the c.net name would no longer be used, international links with ministries that had established strong relationships would continue.

In the autumn of 2004, the final Flying High leaders' conference at Central Hall was held. It served as an opportunity for the leaders present to process the significant changes that were taking place. It was a sorrowful time, marked by many tears, but there was also a strong conviction that something new would emerge from this painful chapter.

Grieving

Locally, the sense of loss continued to be deeply felt. Tony and Hannah had been the cornerstone of our church almost since its inception in 1975. Together, they had been there to guide us through every stage of our development, and then, suddenly, Tony was no longer there. Hannah did, however, continue to be a valued member of our church community until her remarriage to David in 2006.

Graham and his wife, Heather, had also made a significant impact since joining in 1996, forging valuable relationships and contributing greatly to various aspects of church life. Now, they too were not present.

Our Sunday morning worship gatherings became notably subdued. I remember remarking to someone towards the end of the year that we hadn't used drums in worship since that fateful Sunday in June. We were grieving, and like all grief, it required time and needed to be honoured. The focus shifted to God's goodness and faithfulness, with little appetite for high praise and rejoicing.

Plans for the refurbishment of Central Hall were put on hold. The thought of pressing ahead felt overwhelming, especially considering we still needed to raise an additional £400,000 to move forward. No one had the energy to tackle such a daunting task at that moment. As a leadership team, we recognised that if we didn't begin to step up and take hold of our future, the very existence of the church could be at risk.

So, at the start of 2005, we decided it was time to move forward with the refurbishment plans for Central Hall. The trustees, led by Clive Wiseman, and the newly formed Oversight Group played a crucial role in helping us regain our footing, offering invaluable support both in prayer and practical matters. We returned to the congregation, seeking not only their approval for the plans but, more importantly, their financial commitment. The response was incredible. During the first three months of 2005, we set about raising the additional £400,000 needed to kickstart the refurbishment process. Through a combination of one-off gifts, an increase in people's regular giving and a number of interest-free loans, we managed to reach the target required. The trustees then approached the bank to secure the remaining £500,000 required to complete the project, and the bank agreed to lend us the money at a very favourable rate.

This was nothing short of miraculous.

Plans were set in motion to commence refurbishment work at the beginning of June. This would result in the Main Hall being out of service for three months, until the end of August, necessitating alternative arrangements for our Sunday gatherings.

Departures and changes

The shock and sorrow of 2004 proved too much for some, leading to a gradual departure of some individuals from the church. Although their reasons were entirely legitimate, I believe the collective grief played a significant role. We had never encountered this before; we were accustomed to welcoming new members, not receiving yet another call or email informing us that someone was leaving.

Among those who stepped down shortly after this period was Dave Adcock. Dave had been one of the first individuals employed by the church and had served faithfully in various capacities, fostering a culture of warmth and acceptance. He was also instrumental in developing the church's ministry in France. Considering the impending changes to our church leadership shape and structure, I felt a slight reshuffling of responsibilities was in order. However, Dave did not feel the role I proposed was the right fit for him and decided it was time to step down from his leadership position.

Ken Ford, who had been serving as headteacher at The King's School, assumed the role of church pastoral lead. Sue Boniface, a longstanding member of the church, was appointed headteacher at the school. Allan Cox took on the role of missions' leader, while Norma Parrack expanded her role to encompass all aspects of training. Tom Waterton and Ben Hinks moved on from their respective roles in student work and Sublime. Chris Grace, Lou Nynam and Elaine Davidson stepped up to lead Sublime and Tribe, our work among eleven- to fourteen-year-olds, with support from Dave Boniface. Kelvin McMahon was engaged by the Miracle Street team to manage the Red Bus Project, which operated around the city, offering young people a safe space, a place to find a friendly face and a listening ear. Irene Butt, Peter's wife, a great prayer warrior, assumed the role of prayer coordinator and brought fresh impetus to this aspect of church life.

Despite the closure of c.net, Peter Butt's School of Ministries training programme was gaining more traction in many nations across Africa and Asia, and providing great ministry opportunities for many in the UK.

The Northern Congregation continued to explore options for a permanent meeting place and began fundraising for a property, the Beatrice Royal, in Eastleigh. The congregation raised almost £250,000 in pledges and although this was a prolonged and ultimately fruitless endeavour, the process provided valuable lessons.

The years 2004 and 2005 could be described as a period of transition – a movement from one chapter of life to another. But in truth, they were far more than that. These were turbulent, rollercoaster years, filled with deep pain and uncertainty. Yet, through the storms, we found strength in God's mercy and grace. In the midst of the chaos, we experienced his profound comfort and witnessed his divine provision in ways that were nothing short of extraordinary.

Reflections

Writing this chapter has been the hardest part of the book. I am so aware of those that have been affected by Tony's departure, both within Tony's immediate family and in the broader church family. It's not easy to recall these events without a sense of grief and loss. But it would have been dishonest of me to ignore what is, of course, one of the pivotal moments within the life of our church. Not everything that happens in church life is glorious, but we can learn from these darker moments in our story.

I want to end the chapter by honouring Tony and Hannah. Irrespective of what happened, there is no doubt that New Community Church, Southampton, would not exist were it not for their faithful and sacrificial service. Their passion, wisdom and resilience in those early years has seen the wonderful fruit of a life-giving church affecting a community, a city, a nation and the nations. I am forever grateful for the work that they did.

Chapter Twenty

WISDOM AND WORDS

It had been fifteen years since we had ceased our nomadic existence and settled into our new home at Central Hall. Long gone were the days of hauling sound equipment to a hired hall and spending two or three hours setting up and dismantling all that was required for a morning worship gathering. Now, with a sense of anxiety, because of our plans to refurbish the building, we found ourselves on the move once again.

Dispersing

The refurbishment programme started in June 2005, and we decided to hold two smaller Sunday morning meetings at Central Hall. Both took place in the Small Hall, which was largely unaffected by the refurbishment. The first gathering commenced at 9.30 a.m., followed by the second at 11.00 a.m. Meanwhile, our Sublime youth congregation continued meeting on Saturday evenings, and the Sunday Evening Congregation maintained its regular gathering at Central Hall.

Beyond these meetings, we encouraged people to explore several other options. The building we owned in West End, where The King's School met during the week, remained unused on Sundays. Clive and Jane Wiseman offered to host a Sunday gathering there during this period. Additionally, we had developed close ties with two churches within a short distance of Central Hall – James Street Evangelical Church and Orchard Lane Church. Graham and Di Bower, who had previously led Fareham Community Church, a c.net church, had moved to lead the congregation at James Street. The church in Orchard Lane had been a mission church serving the Holyrood Estate for nearly sixty years, with Caroline's aunt and uncle being active members for much of that time. Both churches needed support, so during the refurbishment, we suggested that people consider lending their attendance to these two mission churches. The final option was for members to become more involved with the Flowers Estate gathering at the recently acquired Aster House.

And so, we dispersed for a season while the work was completed on time and on budget under the watchful eye of John Chaffe, a leader from New Forest Community Church and an experienced building surveyor and project manager.

Transitioning from a single large church gathering to several smaller groups for three months during the refurbishment presented both challenges and opportunities.

On the one hand, the shift disrupted our established routines and created some logistical concerns around coordinating venues, maintaining unity and ensuring consistent communication. Some members felt a sense of loss from the larger community dynamic, and it was challenging to recreate the same energy and connection in the smaller settings.

However, this period also offered unique opportunities. The smaller gatherings fostered deeper relationships, provided a more intimate atmosphere for worship, and allowed individuals to participate more actively.

Reopening

In September 2005, Central Hall reopened its doors after a transformative three-month, £1 million refurbishment programme. The project, designed to honour the history of the building while modernising it for future generations, had rejuvenated our 800-seater venue, making it more welcoming, accessible and functional for our community.

The original wooden cinema-style seats, which had graced Central Hall since the 1920s, had been replaced with comfortable fabric seating. The change not only enhanced comfort for our congregation but also brightened the atmosphere of the space, bringing a fresh, modern aesthetic to the historic hall.

One of the most significant changes was the levelling of the floor, which brought the stage much closer to the ground floor level. This adjustment created a more intimate environment, fostering greater connection between the congregation and those leading from the stage. In addition, the imposing 6ft-high wooden barriers that previously separated the ground floor from the tiered seating had been removed, opening up the space and offering a more unified worship experience.

The foyer, too, had undergone a remarkable transformation. The addition of a sleek, modern reception desk made it more welcoming to visitors, while a new lift ensured that the building was fully accessible to those with disabilities. The reopening marked not only the completion of a significant structural renovation but also the beginning of a new chapter in the life of our church.

We hosted a reopening celebration in November for the congregation, building contractors, and invited local church leaders and civic dignitaries. Our friends Delirious? led us in worship, and local leaders, Graham Archer, vicar at Highfield Church, John Risbridger, minister at Above Bar Church and Pete Greig, leader of 24-7 Prayer, shared words of encouragement and challenge.

As our usual Sunday mornings at Central Hall restarted, quite a few of those who had engaged with the smaller congregational settings at James Street, Orchard Lane and Aster House decided that they preferred to stay in those new settings. The group that had been meeting at the school building in West End requested to continue meeting at the building once a month, as they also had enjoyed the smaller, more intimate environment. Because of these factors we began to see a drop-off in numbers attending the main gathering on Sunday morning.

Prophetic word

We had always honoured the prophetic, and from time to time, significant prophetic words would shape us. One of these words, from Sue Singh, part of the leadership team in the Northern Congregation, was delivered around this time:

I saw a picture of a cruise ship, sailing alone in the middle of the ocean. As it sailed, it entered a dense cloud which enveloped the ship, preventing it from seeing where it was going. The cloud transformed into fire and seemed to burn the ship. This burning was changing and reshaping the cruise ship.

This picture is symbolic of where the church is now. The cruise ship represents us, The Community Church. We have had good times, and like a cruise ship, we have spent much of our time on our own enjoyment and pleasure. People have come aboard and enjoyed life, and now they do not want to leave. They have become blind to how the nation has changed around them and to the fact that what they are doing does not reveal Jesus. But God has other plans. He wants to transform us, to refine us so that we can look into the world and know how to be a community that shows Jesus.

After the burning, the ship emerges once more. This time, it has become a fleet of small ships gathered around a warship. The flagship is a warship that carries planes, missiles and weapons to engage in battle with the enemy. It also moves to guard the fleet and prevent casualties. It has fewer people on board. The warship isn't a place for everyone. It is a place for those whom God has called to equip the church. This makes the foundations of The Community Church a place of protection, prayer and safety. Surrounding it are many smaller boats, varying in size. These are fishing boats going into different parts of the sea to catch fish. The smaller fishing boats are protected by the warship. This is their safe place. The fishing boats move back and forth to the warship to be refuelled, to nurture new disciples, and for any casualties of war to be healed and restored.

Most of the people are called to be involved on the fishing boats, sent out to build community in different ways, shapes and sizes. Some of the boats are larger than others – these are the communities we have built in the past and are continuing with (e.g. Eastleigh, Flowers Estate). But others are small, like rowing boats – they are just beginning, catching only one or two fish, but they will grow. As we fish and the ships grow, new captains will emerge, taking on new authority. Some of the fishing boats will become their own warships, sending out their own fishing boats.

There will be some fishing boats that feel capable of standing on their own at this time, but if they go alone, they will sink. They need to remain within the protection of what God is doing and can only go alone when they have become equipped for war. Signs will show when these changes have occurred. God's desire is to breathe His life into us so that we may impact this nation and then go out to other nations.

The challenge for The Community Church at this time is to allow God to burn us and change us into what He envisions. This must be done without us holding on to what God wants to burn away in us. We need to allow Him to design and build His vessels. The Community Church is fragile at the moment, but God is holding us. He wants us as a community of people, but also as individuals, to hear His voice and respond to what He calls us to do and to be. Then the warship and the fishing vessels will be released, bringing community and life to many places in Southampton, the nation and across the world.

This prophetic word felt significant for us as we were navigating the trauma of the departure of Tony and Hannah and Graham and Heather, along with the disruption caused by the refurbishment of Central Hall. We had moved into Central Hall eager to learn how to function as a single apostolic congregation without losing our distinctive value of community. Over the past decade, we had continued to evolve and diversify in our expressions of church, primarily within the building. And now some members of the church were finding a place of belonging in smaller settings. This prophetic word offered us insight into how we could handle this complexity and operate moving forward.

Ireland

In early 2006, the leaders and trustees agreed that I should take a three-month study sabbatical. The past eighteen months had taken their toll on me physically and emotionally, and the time to recharge was a much-appreciated opportunity.

I planned to attend several conferences, visit a few churches to learn from them, read a few books, rest, and in response to another prophetic word, visit Ireland.

My father was Irish, and I had spent my teenage years at secondary school in Northern Ireland. I had left when I was seventeen and had not had occasion to return since. I had recently received three prophetic words from three separate individuals within the space of seven days, all saying the same thing: 'You are to go back to Ireland to rediscover an ancient anointing.' It was an unusual yet incredibly specific word of direction.

When I lived in Northern Ireland, I had an awareness of the Celtic saints and the birth of Christianity in Ireland, but had never engaged with it. Mainly because, as a Protestant in Northern Ireland, the assumption was that anything Celtic was Roman Catholic, and as a 'good' Protestant, it was something we didn't pay much attention to.

My trip to Ireland during this time was incredibly significant. I went with my good friend, Jim, and we decided not to make many plans but to be led by the Spirit, or the 'Wild Goose' as the Celtic saints referred to him. We visited many ancient Celtic sites from the north to the south, learning much about the early Celtic saints and the growth of Christianity in Ireland. On the final day of our trip, we visited the ancient monastery at Clonmacnoise, near Athlone, in the heart of Ireland.

Clonmacnoise is one of Ireland's most significant early Christian monastic sites, founded in AD 544 by St Ciarán, a young priest from the Roscommon area, in response to a prophetic word from his mentor, Enda. Clonmacnoise became a major centre for religion, learning, craftsmanship and trade during the early medieval period.

The site quickly grew in importance due to its strategic location at a crossroads of the river and major land routes.

Monks at Clonmacnoise produced illuminated manuscripts, high crosses and metalwork, contributing to its reputation as a leading intellectual and artistic hub. Over time, the monastery attracted scholars and students from across Ireland and beyond, becoming a burial place for many kings and nobles.

Sitting on a grassy mound next to one of the ruins in Clonmacnoise, I heard the voice of God simply say, 'I'm taking you back to the future.' I sensed there was some learning for me and for the church as to how we should reshape moving forward.

Ancient wisdom

As I delved deeper into early Celtic Christianity, I discovered that the evangelisation of Ireland and the British Isles was profoundly shaped by the monastic movement. These early Christian communities gathered with Christ at their centre, living out their faith through learning, serving and reaching out to those around them. The parish model, which is more familiar to us today, only emerged many centuries later, after most of the population had embraced Christianity. At that point, the parish system became a practical means of organising and providing essential services – baptisms, marriages, funerals and the Eucharist.

However, these early monastic settlements were much more than just religious institutions; they were apostolic communities. Their daily rhythm was one of worship, prayer and work, all deeply rooted in a strong sense of community and service. The people living near these vibrant hubs felt the tangible benefits as these disciples reached out with the gospel, caring for the needy and the sick. These communities also became centres of learning and education and, over time, they grew into centres of commerce and trade.

As people moved closer to these thriving communities, they built homes and, gradually, entire towns and cities began to flourish. In Ireland, many of today's towns that begin with the prefix 'Kil', such as Killarney, Kilbride and Kilbarry, have their origins in these early monastic communities (Kil coming from the original word 'cill', which means 'church'). Similarly, in England, towns with 'minster' in their names, like Wimborne Minster, Westminster and Bedminster, share this heritage.

Reconnecting with this ancient vision became a pivotal moment for me. Taking the time to recharge allowed me to listen more deeply to my heart, and I realised that the weight I carried wasn't solely from Tony's poor decisions regarding his marriage, as heartbreaking as they were. I understood that grace and redemption were always possible if he chose that path. What unsettled me more profoundly was his choice to walk away from the very vision for the church that had shaped most of his life. It planted a seed of doubt – had we all been misled in following his lead?

However, as I embraced new insights and rediscovered the depth of ancient wisdom, my faith and confidence were renewed. I came to understand that the vision we were pursuing didn't originate in 1975, nor in the conferences organised by Arthur Wallis and David Lillie in the 1950s, nor even in AD 544. This vision stretches back to the ancient dream of heaven itself. It was the dream of God dwelling with his people. His people living in true community, growing, learning, flourishing and serving those in need, bringing the reality of God's kingdom to earth, here and now.

Vision casting

Upon returning to Southampton, I shared some of these thoughts with the leadership team – the learning from the ancient monastic movements and the challenge of the 'warship and fishing vessels' prophetic word. We felt that we needed an opportunity to draw a line and cast fresh vision for the future.

For the past fifteen years, we had been focused on learning how to gather and function as one church in one building, but we realised God had already been reshaping us to not only see ourselves as a single congregation meeting at Central Hall, but to simultaneously see how smaller communities across the city could be integrated into this model.

I had been struck again by the Scripture's bias towards the poor, and we sensed that we needed a renewed focus on serving the needs of the most vulnerable people of our city to enable their flourishing.

So, we took the radical decision to draw everyone together for a season in order to cast fresh vision.

Chapter Twenty-one

A New Season

The term 'a new season' is one that is often used in our evangelical and charismatic circles. I recall someone challenging me on this, suggesting that we were in danger of unhelpfully raising people's expectations by continually looking forward to something new. However, as I reflected on the very nature of seasons, I came to the realisation that life itself involves a continuous transition from one season to another. Nature demonstrates this cycle every year, moving from summer to autumn, from winter to spring. This is the cyclical aspect. Yet, each year is not merely a repetition of the last – it's different, which reveals the progression within the cycle.

It follows, then, that it should not be surprising when living organisations and communities pass through times where certain aspects are highlighted more than others. Just as spring is a time for preparation and sowing, summer is associated with growth and harvest, while autumn brings the shedding of what is no longer needed and winter offers a time of quiet and reflection. Each season serves its purpose.

For our church, this was a season to reset.

Reset

The beginning of this new season was to commence on 7th January 2007. The plan was for the entire church community to gather at 7.00 p.m. on Sunday evenings at Central Hall for a period of six months. In the introductory leaflet we produced, we explained:

> Today, we believe our church community stands at the start of a new season in God's purposes. Church is no longer what it used to be. The Spirit of God has brought a fresh freedom and spiritual dynamic, leading to the establishment of hundreds of new churches, and the renewal of scores of others across all traditions. Yet, despite these advancements, the needs of those around us remain as urgent as ever. We believe that we can no longer afford to stay comfortably within the confines of what we call church but must seek more effective ways to bring – and to be – the Good News of Jesus to a world in pain. God has more for us.

We were fortunate to have a magnificent, recently refurbished facility in Central Hall, and we were determined to continue developing it as a centre for gathering, outreach and proclamation of the Good News, as well as enriching our region through the arts, conferences, training and various other events.

Over the years, we had planted numerous congregations to serve specific communities in and around the city. Our aim was not only to resource and strengthen the witness of these congregations, but also to see new and innovative expressions of Church emerge in places where no effective church community currently existed.

While we had already launched several projects to serve and care for our communities, we were acutely aware that we had barely scratched the surface. We felt called to make a deeper contribution to the wellbeing of people in our region, demonstrating the love and kindness of God through an array of caring initiatives.

It would be accurate to say that, following two or three years of disruption, this latest change was not welcomed by everyone. There was much to consider in ensuring that all within our congregations felt connected during this time. The Northern Congregation continued to meet on Sunday mornings in Eastleigh, as did the Flowers congregation at Aster House in Swaythling. The monthly family service at the West End building continued, and several families opened their homes to host smaller gatherings, particularly aimed at those with children. Those who had started supporting the work at James Street Church and Orchard Lane Church continued their involvement there on Sunday mornings but would join us on Sunday evenings.

For members who had been attending the Sublime youth congregation on Saturday evenings, and for those involved in the Sunday Evening Congregation, we organised a café-style gathering from 5.30 p.m. on Sundays ahead of the new evening service.

In anticipation of what we believed God was leading us into, we also decided to change the name of the church from The Community Church Southampton to New Community Church. Previously, we had renamed our charitable company from Cornerstone Network to New Community Network. Now, we wanted to align the work of the charity more clearly with the ministry of the church, ensuring a strong connection with our former identity, while reflecting the vision that God had given us – to be God's new community and to see our communities transformed by the power and love of Christ.

The Big Story

To accompany this new season, I had prepared a teaching series entitled 'The Big Story', based on a phrase found in Luke 24:25-27:

> He said to them, 'How foolish you are, and how slow to believe all that the prophets have spoken! Did not the Messiah have to suffer these things and then enter his glory?' And beginning with Moses and all the Prophets, he explained to them what was said in all the Scriptures concerning himself.

The key phrase that we wanted to focus on was 'beginning with Moses'.

My goal was to show that the Scriptures were not simply a disjointed collection of history, poetry, moral lessons, comforting promises, guiding principles, or material for sermons at weddings and funerals. Rather, the Scriptures are fundamentally a coherent, harmonious, unified account of God's interaction with humanity and his creation. They take us on a journey from God's creative act, through humanity's rebellion, to his plan for the redemption of humankind and all creation, culminating in the ultimate fulfilment of his purposes.

This is often referred to as the 'meta-narrative' or, more simply, the 'big story'.

I wanted to help people see that our story was part of this larger, divine narrative. Our current expression of God's story didn't begin with the formation of the church and its leadership in 1975 but was rooted in this older narrative, the ancient dream of heaven – God dwelling with humanity, men and women sharing their lives in community, expressing and expanding God's rule and reign to the whole of creation.

There was a continuity to the story through the Old Testament all the way to Jesus, the early disciples and to men and women throughout history, right up to the present day. We had been revived and empowered to continue the task of bringing God's kingdom to earth, to be the carriers of the Good News of this kingdom.

We began by looking at the story of Moses in the opening chapters of Exodus. God called Moses in response to the cries of the Israelites, who were suffering in slavery in Egypt. God's answer to their pain was to send a person. Moses, though reluctant at first, did not simply go to proclaim the Good News – he *became* the Good News, bringing the people out from under the oppressive regime of Egypt. As a church, we had previously focused heavily on bringing personal freedom to individuals, but as we explored the Scriptures, it became clear that there was a corporate need as well – systemic strongholds and structures that held people in the grip of sin.

We explored numerous historical examples, from Billy Graham's focus on personal freedom to Martin Luther King Jr's emphasis on social justice; from John Wesley's campaign for both personal and social holiness, to the influence he had on men like William Wilberforce. We also considered modern-day missionaries, like Kelly Greene, a young woman who, in 1999, moved to live in Boy's Town, Nuevo Laredo, Mexico, a walled compound home to 800 prostitutes. These were all people who had been used by God to bring and *be* the Good News.

I then asked the congregation to consider the breadth of the gospel's impact, and what part we each have to play in its proclamation. To those trapped in slavery in Egypt, the Good News was: 'You can be freed from the system that enslaves you.'

In the Gospels, we read the story of Zacchaeus. For him, the Good News was that he could be forgiven and no longer needed his wealth to give his life meaning.

We came to see that Jesus' message is both personal and corporate. If we focus only on the personal, without considering the corporate, then we lose the fullness of the Good News. Conversely, if we live in a society free from oppression and violence, but individuals remain bound in their own sin and guilt, that's not Good News either.

We had, at times, fallen into the trap of perpetuating the divide between the so-called *social gospel* and the *Word-based gospel*. However, as we explored the Scriptures, it became increasingly clear that Jesus' message encompasses both personal and social transformation.

As followers of Jesus, we are all called to *be* and proclaim the Good News of God's kingdom to those in need. The Good News announces, 'Things don't need to be the way they are, there is another way to live.' Every time we respond to the cries of those in pain around us practically or with our words, we are pointing to that alternative kingdom. This response could take the form of feeding a hungry person, listening to someone in crisis, hosting someone in our home, writing to an MP on behalf of another, showing kindness, offering a prayer, bringing reconciliation to a conflict, or lifting someone's spirit. It could be as simple as honouring a commitment, forgiving a wrong, offering comfort to someone in pain, or pointing someone to Christ.

I wanted everyone to understand that they had a part to play in this unfolding story. There needed to be a shift in focus – from what the church could do, to what every member could do as part of God's grand narrative.

Going in

Over the next few months, several events occurred that confirmed God's direction for us.

In March, we invited Chris Kilby and his team to one of our evening meetings. Chris was moving from Winchester to plant a Newfrontiers church in Southampton, and we wanted to welcome and pray for them. During the meeting, Chris shared a prophetic word with us:

God wants you to know that there are no 'no-go' areas for you.

I saw a large area of wasteland bordered by rough coiled barbed wire fencing. On the fencing were poorly made signs, which were badly written too. They were supposed to say 'Keep Out – MINES', but instead, they were spelled more like 'kep awt, miynes', and they were messy too.

I saw many people from New Community Church gathered around the edge of this piece of land, looking in, and then I heard someone say, 'I'm going in', and with that they carefully parted the wire fencing, and crept in.

Once in they could see the tops of the mines protruding from the scrubland. I expected this person to avoid them, but instead, they boldly put forward a foot and stood on one. My natural inclination was to turn away, as their leg would surely be severely damaged. Instead, to my surprise, and to the amazement of all stood around the perimeter fence, instead of a destructive explosion, the mine set off a huge column of coloured streamers that was full of vibrant joy. On seeing this, all those around the fence began to pull it down and enter the wasteland, stamping on mine after mine, and the colours and sound and joy was awesome.

I feel that the area of land represents areas of ministry, or geography that you may historically have thought were areas you were not to get involved in. The thing I felt most clearly was that this exclusion was a work of the enemy. He has tried to keep you out with these poorly written signs. I know they were his handiwork because they were just rubbish. He doesn't have a creative bone in his body, and just tries to twist and mimic that which is good. He is a liar, and the father of lies, and it is a lie that you are not to enter this wasteland.

I felt that the mines were of three main types: sin, sickness and despair. You are to actively stamp on sin wherever its head emerges and see if God doesn't display his 'manifold wisdom' (Ephesians 3:10). You are to actively stamp on sickness and disease wherever you find it and see if God doesn't display his manifold wisdom. You are to actively bring hope into situations of despair and see if God doesn't display his manifold wisdom.

There are no 'no-go' areas for you.

This vision confirmed that there were no off-limits areas of ministry or geography – only places where God's power could break through. It was a wonderful confirmation of all God had been saying to us at that time.

The Community Café

Another significant turning point in our journey took place at our 5:30 p.m. café gathering. Originally, these gatherings were created with the idea of bringing together young people and young adults, offering them a space to connect and share. At first, attendance was sparse, and it seemed like we were still searching for our purpose. However, an unexpected shift occurred that would forever change the nature of our gatherings.

At the end of 2006, we had used Central Hall to provide food for the homeless and those vulnerably housed during the Christmas season. To our surprise, some of those same individuals began showing up at our Sunday afternoon café sessions. It was a turning point we hadn't anticipated, but one we fully embraced. Mat Comer, who was coordinating refreshments at the time, recognised that this was an opportunity to live out our values in a more meaningful way. Considering the teaching we had been reflecting on, it felt only natural – and entirely appropriate – to welcome these guests with open arms – and pizza!

What began as a simple pizza offering – just a few slices for those who walked through our doors – soon grew into something much more significant. As we continued to welcome our guests, our team's passion for hospitality and compassion deepened. We realised that this café gathering could be more than a casual event; it could be a lifeline for those in need.

This was the humble beginning of what is now known as the Community Café. It has since blossomed into a vital weekly event, running every Sunday without fail. Over the years, we have served tens of thousands of meals to those who need them most. While we initially started with a simple gesture – offering a slice of pizza – our vision has grown to include complete meals, with wholesome main courses and desserts, ensuring that everyone who comes through our doors is treated to something more than just food; they're offered kindness, warmth and a sense of community.

Looking back, we see how this transformation has reflected our journey as a team and a church community. What started as a small effort has turned into a vital part of who we are, and every meal we serve now represents not only the nourishment of the body but the fostering of connection and care. The Community Café stands as a testament to the power of opening our doors, hearts and kitchens to those in need.

The Big Story and the Community Café were change moments for us as a church. The third and probably most significant event needs its own chapter.

Chapter Twenty-two

EDUCATION, EDUCATION, EDUCATION

In September 1982, we had established The King's School at our West End building. Over time, the school grew, providing education for children from primary through to secondary level. We even acquired a second property on the outskirts of the city to house The King's School Senior.

By 1992, the church's involvement with the senior school ceased, as the Hampshire Christian Education Trust took responsibility for the secondary element of The King's School. By 2005, Sue Boniface had taken up the position of headteacher for The King's Primary School. However, we began to find it increasingly difficult to bear the financial burden, compounded by the fact that fewer and fewer families from our church were sending their children to the school. After months of reflection and numerous conversations, we made the significant decision to re-merge The King's Primary School with The King's School Senior under the governance of the Hampshire Christian Education Trust. This marked the end of our governance and financial responsibility for the school.

It seemed, then, that in 2006, our direct involvement in education had come to an end, when the administration of the school was formally transferred.

Oasis Community Learning

During my sabbatical that same year, I spent a day with Steve Chalke, founder of the Oasis charity, which had recently set up Oasis Community Learning and had begun opening schools funded by the government. The running of schools by Christian organisations had been a key part of the Church's mission for hundreds of years and was still a main part of its strategy in overseas mission. However, since the Education Act of 1902, local authorities had been given responsibility to provide education for all young people. But a recent shift in government policy saw the creation of new academies, which provided local communities, parent and charity groups with the opportunity to serve their areas in a transformative way. I was intrigued as to how they operated and asked Steve if I could spend some time learning from him. He graciously invited me to visit one of the academies being set up in Bristol. The vision of Oasis Community Learning was to establish Christ-centred community hubs in some of the most challenging areas of the nation. What I witnessed left me deeply inspired.

That autumn, I invited Steve to speak with our leadership team about this vision. He emphasised a holistic approach to community transformation, drawing inspiration from Jewish communities, where the home functions as the centre of community life. It is where the family gathers to eat, worship, play, study and work. Yet, in modern Western society, we have compartmentalised these activities into separate spaces. Steve's vision was to create a more integrated approach, with the school acting as a hub where children, families and the broader community could find belonging, support, learning and faith.

We enquired about the possibility of establishing something similar in Southampton but, at the time, it wasn't feasible.

Fast forward a year to January 2007.

We had begun our teaching series on The Big Story, which emphasised the importance of the entire Church engaging with culture – being and bringing Good News, proclaiming the gospel, and responding to the needs in our community.

Around March, I received a phone call from Steve. He had been approached by the government, asking if Oasis would be interested in entering a bidding process to open two new academies in Southampton. The City Council had recently completed a review of secondary schools, deciding to close four existing institutions – two on the west side of the city and two on the east – and reopen two new ones. Government policy at the time required interested parties to enter a bidding process, after which Southampton City Council would decide who would be entrusted with the responsibility to operate the new schools.

Steve asked if we would be willing to serve as local partners for Oasis Community Learning. If we were on board, Oasis would proceed with the bid, but if not, they would withdraw from the process. Given the direction we had been developing regarding city engagement and transformation, we saw this as a remarkable opportunity.

Coalition

We formed a coalition of local partners, including the Winchester Diocese Education Board, the YMCA and ourselves as New Community Network, drawing on our twenty-plus years of involvement in education.

Adrian Thomas led the creation of a detailed bid, combining the expertise of the coalition, and our own understanding of the local communities. We presented to various bodies – the City Council, the local education team, the leadership of the existing schools, parents and the local community. There were three other bidders: two national academy providers with no local partners, and a local consortium, whom we knew to be the City Council's preferred choice and front-runners. And then there was us.

As the presentations progressed, it became evident that we were not the favourite. The local Southampton consortium had the inside track. Their challenge, however, was that their bid did not come with the guaranteed government funding that the academy chains, including Oasis Community Learning, could secure to build a new school facility.

Then something remarkable happened – what some might call a miracle.

The election miracle

On 3rd May, the local council elections took place. The results were extraordinarily close, and no party had the majority to form a cabinet. The Conservative Party had performed better than expected, securing eighteen seats. Labour also won eighteen seats, while the Liberal Democrats secured twelve. For the previous five years, the Liberal Democrats had held power, and before that, the Labour Party had controlled the council for thirteen years. Normally, an agreement would have been reached between the Liberal Democrats and Labour to determine who would lead the council. However, strong disagreements arose between the two, and the Conservatives put forward their leader, Alec Samuels, as a candidate for the council's leadership. This seemed improbable until one Liberal Democrat councillor, Norah Goss, broke party ranks and voted in favour of a Conservative administration, while her colleagues abstained.

This was significant because the Conservative councillors had been highly supportive of our bid throughout the consultative process. They had expressed concerns over the viability of the Southampton-based bid, viewing it as, up to that point, the Liberal Democrat controlled local authority under another guise.

It was therefore a surprise to many, including us, that at the City Council Cabinet meeting on 2nd July, it was agreed that the two new schools would be awarded to Oasis Community Learning, supported by local partners: New Community Network, YMCA and the Winchester Diocese Education Board.

A seat at the table

This decision catapulted us into a completely new level of visibility and influence within the city. I described it as suddenly 'having a seat at the table'. For many years, as a Christian community, it had felt like we were outsiders, watching from the fringes as decisions were made in the corridors of power. Now, through our involvement in education, we had been invited in, which had significant implications for the way the church would interact with the City Council.

Along with the prophetic confirmation from Chris Kilby, the unexpected and unplanned prospect of serving those in material need with regular hot meals, and now the chance to work alongside Oasis Community Learning in providing Christ-centred education for hundreds of young people, all signalled that God was propelling us in a very clear direction.

If I were to summarise this shift, it would be the movement away from a focus solely on praying for a great revival, as had been a strong emphasis for many years, and an increasing expectation leading up to the year 2000, towards a recognition that God had been reviving his Church and now it was our responsibility as revived and empowered individuals to step out in our God-given authority to see the manifestation of God's kingdom in the present, across all spheres of our communities. This wasn't new; it had been the hallmark of the early days of our church as we had ventured into education, health care and the business world.

I had read a lot about the great Evangelical Awakening of the eighteenth century that saw the birth of Methodism under the leadership of John and Charles Wesley. After fifty years of ministry, some would say 'revival', the number of Methodists numbered around 70,000 at the time of John Wesley's death in 1791. The church had been revived with not only thousands of Methodist societies across the nation but scores of Anglicans who now aligned with Wesley and described themselves as Evangelical. It was as these 'revived' men and women began to engage in the challenges of their day that Great Britain experienced dramatic social transformation.

This was the time of the great reformers who tackled everything from education for all, to workers' rights, to penal reform, to animal rights and to the abolition of slavery.

The evidence of the last thirty years, it could be argued, was that we were already living in revival. The church today was unrecognisable from its state in the 1960s and 1970s – there was vibrancy, life, healing and joy, with many finding freedom from legalistic religious practices.

Surely, *this* is what revival looks like?

We had prayed for revival. Many had prophesied revival. But what if we had already been witnessing revival since the very start of our church's journey? And what if the extra blessings received through the ministry of John Wimber, the influence of Toronto and Bill Johnson and Bethel were the 'times of refreshing' referenced in Acts 3:19?

There had been many who had grown disillusioned with the constant revival rhetoric of the 1990s, and had walked away from church because expectations of a great ingathering hadn't happened as they had hoped. But I was convinced that if we only focused on the initial dramatic element of revival – mass conversions – and failed to ask the question, 'What should we do once we had been revived?' then we failed to embrace the fullness of the story of God as revealed in the Scriptures.

And now, it wasn't enough to remain on our 'cruise liner', enjoying the blessings of revival. It was time to take seriously the call to allow God to transform us into a 'warship', accompanied by a 'flotilla of fishing vessels', to step into those minefields, bringing life to the city, as demonstrated by the great reformers of the eighteenth and nineteenth centuries.

The new term

At the end of those six months, we outlined what the new term, starting in September, would look like. Sunday morning meetings at Central Hall would resume, but we encouraged those who had found a place of purpose and belonging in the smaller gatherings to remain there, and we coined a new generic term for the emerging congregations and groups with a local mission focus: core communities.

These core communities would be supported by a pastoral framework, a new training initiative with three teaching tracks – Love of the Word, Spiritual Formation and Ministry and Mission – as well as a network of spiritual mentors.

Sim Dendy, who had moved with his family from Littlehampton, had been employed to oversee the use of the various buildings we were using – Central Hall, Aster House, West End, James Street and Orchard Lane – to better serve the community. These venues would provide counselling, advice and services that proclaimed the 'shalom' of God. We would be referring to these as Life Centres.

At Central Hall, we decided to create and open a coffee shop for both public use and internal meetings. Our goal was to revive the original vision of our Methodist forefathers when they opened the building in the 1920s: to be a 'busy hive of positive ideals'. Plans were made to transform a corridor into a warm and welcoming space with direct access to the street.

One initiative that came to an end during this time was The Sanctuary project, providing accommodation for vulnerable men. The way local authority funding worked meant that they were unable to continue to fund the work and so we reluctantly agreed to close the facility.

A good city to grow old in and a good city to grow up in

We had also come to realise that the task of bringing life to the city was not solely through church-organised activities, but through everyone contributing to their everyday roles, whether in their workplaces or communities. This truth hit home one Sunday evening when we were praying for orphaned children we were supporting in Kenya. I glanced to my left and saw David and Anna Wright. They ran Paint Pots nursery schools, caring for more than 1,000 children across eight schools in Southampton. Yet, we had never mentioned them or prayed for them.

We began to highlight different people who were serving in various capacities throughout the city. One member of our congregation was the cabinet member for Children's Services, another was the head of parenting for the city. Many of our congregation were schoolteachers, doctors, nurses and health professionals. Others were business owners, and some were stay-at-home parents. Our aim was to help everyone recognise that they were part of God's mission, not only in the church but in the city at large.

A passage from Zechariah 8:3-5 particularly resonated with us. In the NIV, the verses say:

> This is what the LORD says: 'I will return to Zion and dwell in Jerusalem. Then Jerusalem will be called the Faithful City, and the mountain of the LORD Almighty will be called the Holy Mountain.'

> This is what the LORD Almighty says: 'Once again men and women of ripe old age will sit in the streets of Jerusalem, each of them with cane in hand because of their age. The city streets will be filled with boys and girls playing there.'

But in *The Message* version, it reads:

> I've come back to Zion; I've moved back to Jerusalem. Jerusalem's new names will be Truth City, and Mountain of GOD-of-the-Angel-Armies, and Mount Holiness.

> A Message from GOD-of-the-Angel-Armies: Old men and old women will come back to Jerusalem, sit on benches on the streets and spin tales, move around

safely with their canes – a good city to grow old in. And boys and girls will fill the public parks, laughing and playing – a good city to grow up in.

We were struck by the vision of 'a good city to grow old in' and 'a good city to grow up in'. This, we realised, is what it looks like when God's kingdom is manifested in a city. We used these verses to inspire every member to see the role they played in bringing this vision to reality. We had prayed, 'Your kingdom come', and now we had a tangible vision of what that might look like.

You can imagine our astonishment, then, when in late 2007, the Southampton Strategic Partnership – a group representing all sectors of the city community – published its twenty-year vision for the city with the opening statement:

> ... Southampton will be known as a city that is good to grow up in and good to grow old in, where people are proud to live ...

God was not only resetting our vision but aligning it with a broader vision for the city, presenting us with an extraordinary opportunity to partner with the future he was unfolding.

Chapter Twenty-three

NEW PARTNERS

Our first gathering back at Central Hall on the morning of 2nd September 2007 was, in many ways, a bittersweet experience. It marked the beginning of a new chapter for us as a church, but it also highlighted some of the challenges we were yet to face.

As I stood in the hall, a place that had once been brimming with life, it was hard not to notice how much things had changed. The room, which only a few years before had held around 600 people on a regular basis, now felt emptier than ever before. We probably had no more than 200 people in attendance that morning, and while we had expected smaller numbers, the reality of it was still difficult to process.

The weight of the task

The reasons for the low attendance were varied and understandable. We had released people to continue supporting the smaller, local community gatherings that had sprung up across various parts of the city. These gatherings, on the Flowers Estate, Orchard Lane and James Street, were integral to our outreach and mission work, providing a more intimate and local expression of faith. The West End group had moved from meeting monthly at The King's School building to meeting weekly. At the same time, the students who would normally fill many of the seats of Central Hall had not yet returned to the city following the summer break. Additionally, there were some who had chosen to move on, following the trauma and turmoil of the past couple of years, and others who hadn't fully bought into the reset of vision that we felt so strongly about.

As I surveyed the scene, the weight of the task ahead became clear. At lunch that day, I turned to Caroline, and with a hint of humour masking my true emotions, I said, 'I have the title for the book I'm going to write: "Honey, I shrunk the church!"'

Though said in jest, there was a deeper truth to the statement. We had, in many ways, been diminished. But we were convinced, beyond any doubt, that the direction we felt God leading us was the right one. I had preached often on the journey of faith that people like Abram and others had embarked on. We have the benefit of hindsight to see that their steps of obedience worked out in the end. But when you are in that moment, when the story is still unfolding, it can feel a little scary. We had decided to move in a certain direction, we had received some encouragement that this was the right step to take; however, the evidence now before us seemed to be saying the opposite. It was a struggle for a while to keep the team and the congregations, particularly those who had returned to Central Hall, encouraged and focused on the vision for the future.

We realised that now the real work had to begin, and we knew that we couldn't do it alone. We needed God's help, of course, but we also needed the support and wisdom of others to navigate this new path.

The year 2008 brought a new wave of challenges, this time in the form of financial difficulties. Despite our best efforts, the financial pressures we faced meant that for the first time in the church's history, we were forced to make some roles redundant. It was a painful decision, one that weighed heavily on our hearts, but we had no other option. Ken Ford, who had served as the director of Pastoral Care for two years, had his role come to an end. It was a difficult moment, as Ken had provided incredible care and leadership during a tumultuous time. Likewise, after twenty-four years of dedicated service, Phil Orchard's role as an employed leader also ended. Phil had been a cornerstone of the church for more than two decades, and his departure felt like the end of an era. Finally, Paul Gander, who had been our buildings and maintenance manager, was another significant loss. These three individuals had each played vital roles in the life of our church, and their departure left a noticeable gap.

In addition to these redundancies, we saw further changes in leadership. Theo Amer, who had been leading the Evening Congregation, decided to pursue a lifelong ambition to become a commercial airline pilot and enrolled in a training programme. We were sad to see him go, but we fully supported his decision, recognising the calling on his life. Similarly, Dave

Boniface, who had led the Sublime youth congregation, felt that his time in the role had come to a natural end. It was a difficult season, marked by the loss of key individuals from our team, and at times it felt like we were being stripped back to the bare essentials.

New beginnings *again*

However, as is often the case, amid the endings came new beginnings. Adrian Thomas, who had served as our finance manager and then business manager, was offered a part-time role to assist in the opening of the two new Oasis academies. His experience and wisdom were invaluable during this time of transition. Mark Iles, one of our existing leaders and a qualified accountant, took on the role of finance manager, stepping into the role with great competence. Allan Cox, who had been faithfully serving the church for many years, broadened his responsibilities to include oversight of our work in France, with a specific brief to determine the future of Sans Frontières, our house in Normandy. His strategic thinking and calm leadership were a blessing during this season of uncertainty.

Sim Dendy, who had moved from Littlehampton with a vision to develop the use of the various buildings we had access to, took on a wider role within the congregation that met on Sunday mornings at Central Hall. His energy and enthusiasm were infectious, and he brought a fresh perspective to the way we utilised our resources.

And then, as if by divine appointment, other new partners began to emerge.

Since the closure of c.net in 2004, in the four years since then, we had been operating as an independent church. This was quite a shift for us, as we had always been part of a wider national and international network. There were advantages to this independence. We were able to focus almost 100 per cent of our efforts on the work of the church in the city, without the 'distraction', as some would call it, of the broader ministry. However, there was also a downside – it could feel quite lonely at times. The sense of isolation, of being untethered from a larger community, was palpable. We missed the camaraderie and support that came from being part of something bigger than ourselves.

Around this time, Caroline and I were invited to do some work with the Pioneer national leadership team. Pioneer, like c.net, was a national and international network that had emerged during the early days of the charismatic and new church movements of the 1970s and 1980s. Led by Gerald Coates, a prominent national figure, Pioneer had a strong reputation across the UK. However, they were going through a challenging time as a network. The early enthusiasm and momentum that had characterised their growth had begun to wane, and there was a growing sense of disillusionment among some within the movement. Additionally, there was a divergence of vision and direction within the leadership, which was creating tension.

Over the course of 2007 and 2008, Caroline and I met with the Pioneer team every three or four months. Our role was to offer support, advice and perspective as outside consultants. We felt that we had something valuable to contribute, given our own experiences with c.net and the challenges of leading a church through difficult transitions. As the months passed, we began to sense that we had done all we could do. By the end of 2008, the network seemed to be in a much healthier place, and we felt that our time as consultants was coming to an end. However, just as we were preparing to step away, Gerald Coates announced that he felt his time as leader of the network had come to an end. He believed that the network needed fresh leadership to move forward, and various conversations took place about who might be best suited for the role.

At what we thought would be our final meeting with the network leadership team, a surprising proposal was made. John Noble, a close friend of Gerald and a fellow leader in Pioneer, quite out of the blue spoke up and suggested Caroline and me as potential candidates to lead. We all laughed at the proposal and the meeting closed without any conclusion being made. As we drove from the meeting to a local restaurant, Caroline and I reflected on John's proposal and thought how strange it would be if that's what happened. As we sat at dinner later that evening, Gerald turned to us both and said, 'When John Noble mentioned your names something leapt in my spirit, and I think you are the next leaders of Pioneer.'

We were as shocked as anyone, but Gerald expressed his confidence in us, encouraging us to consider the offer seriously. It was an unexpected turn of events, and one that we did not take lightly.

After a period of reflection, prayer and discussion with the leaders at New Community Church, we concluded that this was an opportunity we should accept. The role felt like a natural fit with our personal sense of calling, and it would reposition the church once again at the heart of a national and international network. And so, the process of transitioning into the leadership of Pioneer began.

Stronger relationships

Meanwhile, back in Southampton, there was an existing Pioneer church – City Life Church. We had always had a good relationship with them, though it wasn't necessarily any stronger than our relationships with other churches in the city. However, given that we were about to take on the national leadership of the Pioneer network, it seemed absurd that we didn't have a closer connection with this local Pioneer church. And so, we began meeting with the leadership of City Life Church to explore what a greater collaborative approach might look like.

As we spent time together, it became clear that there was a great deal of synergy between us. Our visions aligned, and our approaches to ministry were remarkably similar. As we delved into the history of our respective churches, we discovered that both New Community Church and City Life Church had been birthed around the same time, in the early 1970s. There was even a point in the late 1970s when the leadership of both churches had considered merging. However, in the end, City Life chose to align themselves with Gerald Coates and the emerging Pioneer network, while we went in a different direction. Now, decades later, our paths were converging once again.

Over the course of the next few years, we hosted regular joint gatherings at Central Hall, combining leadership development groups, supporting each other's projects and meeting together as leaders. We even went so far as to jointly employ two members of staff for a period. Bev Webb, who co-led City Life Church, took on the role of part-time pastoral lead for New Community Church, and Dan Pooley was jointly employed as a student worker serving both church communities.

Through our connections with City Life Church, we were introduced to Carl Wills, a prophetic figure based in Salisbury. Carl had been going through what he described as a 'wilderness season', a time of waiting and uncertainty. However, our connection with him reignited a passion and vision that he had been carrying for some time. He began travelling regularly to Southampton, bringing with him a fresh sense of the prophetic and a clear calling to pray for the church, the city and the region. His input was catalytic, helping to reawaken our awareness of the Holy Spirit's work among us.

Another significant moment came in 2009 when we attended a conference hosted by another church in our building, Central Hall, where Bill Johnson from Bethel Church in California was speaking. The conference was a turning point for us, not just in terms of leadership, but for the entire church. We had always believed in the power and presence of the Holy Spirit, but what we experienced at the conference took that understanding to a new level. Bill Johnson spoke about the importance of hosting the presence of God, of creating space for the Holy Spirit to move in both our individual lives and corporate gatherings. His teachings resonated deeply with us and gave us a renewed sense of purpose and vision.

Repentance

Later that year, another profound moment came when we hosted an event with Mark Stibbe and Marc Dupont. Mark Stibbe was at that time the vicar of a large charismatic Anglican Church, St Andrew's, Chorleywood, and Marc Dupont was a recognised prophetic minister who had been very involved with the meetings in Toronto that sparked the Toronto Blessing movement.

I was introducing one of the sessions when both Mark and Marc approached the platform and asked for the microphone. I had no idea what they were proposing to do. They both got on their knees at the front of the hall and announced that they felt they needed to repent to us as a church. We were still unsure as to what was coming.

'We need to repent to you, New Community Church, on behalf of two fathers who are no longer present.' Mark Stibbe continued, 'I want to repent on behalf of the apostolic father of this house who left you.'

Marc Dupont then proceeded to repent on behalf of the prophetic father.

As Mark and Marc knelt and began their heartfelt confessions, the room shifted from quiet anticipation to a powerful atmosphere of raw emotion. Initially, there was confusion; no one expected this moment of repentance.

The deep sincerity in their voices, together with the symbolic act of kneeling, broke through the silence, and it became clear that this was not just an apology; it was a moment of reconciliation and healing for the entire church.

For many in the room, the words opened old wounds, yet they also seemed to provide the very balm needed for healing. Emotions began to surface – some with tears welling up, others quietly bowing their heads in reflection and prayer. A collective sense of release seemed to flow through the congregation as years of unspoken pain and abandonment were finally acknowledged.

The tension melted into an overwhelming sense of unity and grace. Some in the audience wept openly, while others embraced those beside them, as the weight of past hurts gave way to a shared moment of forgiveness. There was a palpable shift in the room – something deeper than words, as though an unseen burden had been lifted from the congregation as a whole.

The connection with Bill Johnson and the Bethel Church and moments like these were God's gifts to us, bringing fresh faith and healing to our hearts, enabling us to move forward with greater confidence.

Our partnership with Pioneer flourished, and the new connections we had formed with leaders in the city and across the UK strengthened our sense of being part of something much larger than ourselves. We had come through a season of loss and stripping back, but in its place, God had brought restoration, healing and new life.

The journey was far from over, but we had a renewed confidence in the God who redeems, restores and rebuilds. Looking back on those years, I can now see how each twist and turn, each loss and gain, had been part of a greater plan. The church had indeed been 'shrunk', but in doing so, we had been positioned for something far greater than we could have imagined.

Chapter Twenty-four

LOVE AND BUSES

A recurring pattern throughout the history of our church has been the dynamic nature of leadership and transitions within leadership across the church. While a core group of leaders have remained consistent over the years, I often wished for a more stable and settled broader team. However, being an apostolic community means constant movement – people arriving, serving, contributing, and then moving on. Some join us for a season, offering their unique gifts before transitioning to other contexts. Others are raised within the community, only to eventually move on for a variety of reasons.

Double-decker bus

It's also true of the congregation. We have always had a strong and consistent core, many of whom have been around since the first meeting and others who have been part of the church for thirty or forty years. And then there are others who join the church, maybe as students, or because of work, and then, when their course or placement finishes, they move on. We see it as a privilege to be able to serve people in this way.

I once received a prophetic word that I was like the driver of a double-decker bus. The bus had a clear destination in mind but as with any bus journey, the route meanders through estates and shopping areas, rather than travelling directly to the destination, which you would do if you were driving in a car. The person who gave me the word went on to say that the bus would stop at each bus stop, where some people would get off and others would get on. 'This is how you and the church are called to operate, helping people in their own individual journeys, some getting on for a season, others getting off.' We had to learn to be comfortable with this coming and going.

This pattern became especially evident again in the years following our vision reset.

Carl Wills and his wife, Mel, relocated to Southampton just as Mark Simpson, a young pastor from South Africa, felt called by God to join our church and wider ministry. Mark, along with his family, arrived the same week as Carl and Mel. Around this time, Theo completed his training and made the important decision to forgo a career as a commercial airline pilot, instead stepping into the role of director of Community Life at Central Hall. Simultaneously, Adam Clewer, who had grown up in our youth congregation, Sublime, and had been serving as a youth pastor in nearby New Milton, was appointed to lead our Next Generation ministry.

At the same time, Lynn Swart, who had faithfully served in worship both locally and internationally for more than two decades, felt called to move on, and accepted a role at a thriving church in Manchester. Michael and Amanda Thom, members of our church since 2004 and leaders at the Orchard Lane Church, agreed to relocate to France to serve as hosts at the Sans Frontières house in Normandy. Additionally, Bryn and Sue Singh were appointed as the new leaders of the Eastleigh congregation, allowing Allan and Liz Cox to dedicate more time to ministry across the city and the nation.

Inspired by Mark Stibbe's book *Breakout*,[9] we began working collaboratively with City Life Church, developing several new missional communities. Mark's story of a church rediscovering a Spirit-empowered, New Testament model of church mission deeply resonated with us. St Andrew's, Chorleywood had been a leading force in church renewal for more than three decades, and in the last five years, had seen tremendous growth as the congregation transitioned from a centralised model to one where mission-shaped communities of up to fifty people met in schools, community centres, coffee shops and other venues.

This vision aligned with the prophetic word we received about 'warships and fishing vessels', and we were excited to explore these new possibilities with our friends and partners.

In addition to the existing communities meeting at Central Hall, West End, Eastleigh, James Street, Orchard Lane and the Flowers Estate, we established new missional communities. These included one linked with the Community Café, which we called The Streets, another group serving the Polish community, one for the Nepalese, and two café churches at the Oasis academies. We also launched Tea Break at the Cobbett Road Library in Bitterne Park to connect with and serve the elderly in that area. It was a season of innovation and experimentation. Some communities thrived, while others struggled to gain traction.

Engaging

Beyond these new groups, we explored other ways to engage with our communities. We had been gifted two residential properties in recent years through various means and had been using them to house vulnerable people. This led to the formation of New Community Housing, a group tasked with managing these properties. Additionally, we established New Community Health in partnership with a local General Practitioner, with the aim of developing holistic health and wellbeing initiatives. Both ventures were experimental, and neither developed as we had initially hoped. We eventually sold the properties and reinvested the funds in our ongoing mission among those in need in our local community.

One intriguing development during this time was our growing partnership with the Methodist Church. Inspired by Nicky Gumbel's vision at Holy Trinity Brompton to repurpose disused Anglican church buildings across the nation, and a pastor from Chicago who revitalised declining churches by adding resources and leadership, we began to consider how we could keep such church communities alive in Southampton.

We had long been inspired by our Methodist forefathers, who had the original vision for Central Hall. We saw ourselves as continuing the mission that these pioneers began eighty years ago. By the end of the Second World War, there were more than fifty Methodist churches in the Southampton Circuit, but by 2010, fewer than twenty remained.

Unexpectedly, I was contacted by a local Methodist minister who informed me that the Circuit was considering disposing of several buildings. He asked if we would be interested in partnering with them to keep these churches open. This opportunity was both surprising and welcome. We negotiated with the Circuit leadership for City Life Church and the Flowers Estate core community to use Swaythling Methodist Church, located near the university. The small congregation that had been meeting there agreed to refurbish one of the smaller rooms, freeing up the main auditorium and other spaces for our use.

Paul Woodman, leader at City Life Church, formed a team to run a Messy Church and youth club at St Andrew's Methodist Church in Sholing – situated at the heart of the city's east side, near the site of one of the Oasis academies. The existing Methodist congregation would merge with another nearby church, Woolston Methodist, giving our core community full access to the building throughout the week and on Sundays. At Easter 2014 the group meeting weekly at the West End building would also relocate to the St Andrew's building.

This partnership flourished and led to meetings with the general secretary of the Methodist Church in London. The general secretary endorsed our innovative approach and encouraged similar collaborations between Pioneer churches and Methodist congregations across the nation.

Love Southampton

Our close collaboration with City Life Church, Oasis Community Learning and the Methodists began to model what true partnership could look like. Paul Woodman, co-leader of City Life Church, was appointed chaplain to the Oasis academies, and together, in my role as chair of the Academy Council, we began engaging more broadly across the city. It was the time of austerity, when local authority funding was being cut. Paul and I met with Clive Webster, the director of Children's Services, to explore how the church could support the city.

Clive highlighted three areas where help was urgently needed: fostering and adoption, youth provision and pre-school services. At that time, the local authority needed to recruit eighty more foster parents. Youth services were being slashed due to budget cuts, and pre-school provision, although essential, was underfunded.

Our meeting with Clive also revealed the city's confusion about how the church was organised and who they should approach for assistance, if required. We explained that the church in Southampton comprised several networks, including the Southampton Christian Network, Churches Together, the Anglican Deanery, the Methodist Circuit and the Roman Catholic Diocese, as well as the Southampton Pastors Network representing minority churches.

Afterwards, Paul and I met with the Bishop of Southampton, Jonathan Frost, and we agreed that an umbrella organisation was needed to unify these groups and facilitate communication with the City Council. This led to the formation of Love Southampton. A board was formed consisting of key leaders from various denominations and networks, including the Anglican bishop, Rt Rev. Jonathan Frost, the Roman Catholic dean, Father Vincent Harvey, two representatives from the Southampton Pastors Network, Dr John-Paul Oddoye and Pastor Michael Olutoye, the Methodist Circuit Superintendent, Rev. Terry Hudson, the co-leader of City Life Church, Bev Webb, the city centre URC minister, Rev. Sarah Hall, chair of the Southampton Christian Network, Pastor Paul Finn and myself.

Paul Woodman then formed a steering group that drew together individuals and organisations that were already addressing the city's immediate needs.

The atmosphere at Central Hall was electric as more than 400 people gathered for the launch of Love Southampton in early 2014 – a bold initiative aimed at uniting churches, civic leaders and the broader community to tackle some of the city's most pressing needs. Among the attendees were key church leaders, local officials and passionate members of churches from across the city, all eager to explore ways they could make a meaningful impact. The event sparked a series of conversations that would soon birth transformative initiatives, grounded in the shared desire to see the city flourish.

Families for Forty

One of the first tangible expressions of this shared vision came through the Families for Forty campaign, an ambitious effort to recruit forty new foster families. The prophetic team at City Life Church, inspired by the vision, created a stunning work of art: a symbolic piece featuring forty intricate, ornate keys – each representing a family that would unlock hope and stability for a child in need. This prophetic artwork became a powerful symbol of commitment and was later presented to the City Council's cabinet member for Children's Services during a special event, solidifying the partnership between the church and the city's leadership.

Over the next two years, through community open evenings, information sessions held in churches, and a vital partnership with the Home for Good charity, the campaign achieved its goal. Forty new families opened their homes and hearts to children, providing not just foster care, but a future filled with love and security.

Expanding support for youth

But fostering was only the beginning. As the movement grew, so did the recognition of the needs among the city's youth. In an extraordinary effort to reach marginalised young people, we gathered and united twenty youth workers from across the city, bringing them together to strategise and share ideas. These dedicated individuals were working in some of Southampton's most underserved areas, including the newly established Oasis academies in Mayfield and Lordshill. Here, youth workers were positioned to engage with students, offering support, mentorship and guidance to those who needed it most.

In Sholing, on a council housing estate, a unique opportunity arose: the use of a vacant shop unit, previously a City Council youth drop-in centre. This space, teeming with potential, became the base of operations for the newly appointed full-time youth worker from St Mary's Anglican church. Their mission was to build connections with the local youth, offering a safe space for community, conversation and growth. From this simple shop unit, the Monty's Community Hub was born – an initiative that continues to serve as a beacon of hope and opportunity for young people in the area.

Supporting families and young children

Recognising that transformation starts early, we also turned our attention to pre-school provision, a critical foundation for healthy family life. Bringing together the leaders of around eighty pre-school groups run by churches across the city, we formed a new collaborative group. In partnership with the City Council, this group began working to support parents and young children during those formative early years. Through their efforts, they provided vital resources, guidance and community, helping families navigate the challenges of early childhood with confidence and care.

Jubilee

The year 2014 was also the fiftieth anniversary of Southampton's city status. In England the term 'city' can only be used to describe a centre of population if it has a cathedral.

However, from time to time the Monarch can confer the status of 'city' on a given town because of its growing importance to the region. Because of the population growth of recent years, the economic importance of the port and the long history of public administration, Southampton was granted city status on 24th February 1964, by royal charter.

In line with the encouragement in Jeremiah 29:7 to 'seek the peace and prosperity of the city to which I have carried you' we decided to host a joint church service at the city centre Anglican church, St Mary's, and invite civic dignitaries, church leaders and charity leaders to pray for the city.

We used the idea of Jubilee, a biblical concept that refers to a special year, occurring every fiftieth year, where debts were forgiven, slaves were freed and land was returned to its original owners. It was meant to promote social justice, economic reset and equality within the community of Israel.

We decided to craft a declaration that we would read out as a prophetic statement over the city:

A Jubilee Declaration for Southampton

In this year of Jubilee, we proclaim liberty to the people of Southampton and the surrounding towns and villages. A year when debts are cleared, chains of oppression are broken, inheritance is restored, and we experience unprecedented harvest. We speak blessing over this city and declare that every area will be touched by God's love.

Southampton will be known as a great place to grow up and a great place to grow old. Young and old will walk the streets in safety.

We declare freedom from every form of injustice. This will be a city where crime is reduced, and we see an end to violence and bloodshed. This will be a city known for faithfulness, truth and justice. Where everyone has the opportunity to learn and grow to become all that God has created them to be. A city of shelter for the refugee and stranger, where the orphan and the lonely are placed in families.

We declare that this city will become a place of development, employment and industry. A city that will attract international investment and businesses that will operate with integrity, where creative solutions will be found for the city's challenges. We proclaim health and healing, peace and prosperity, freedom and creativity.

We declare that this will be a city where Christ is honoured, and many people will turn to God. A city that honours its history, respects its environment and leaves a legacy for generations to come.

The God who has been Our Help in Ages Past will be our hope for the future!

Amen!

The final line referred to the famous hymn by Isaac Watts, a son of Southampton, which is still played from the Civic Centre clock tower every day at midday. It is a constant reminder that others have gone before us with the same heart and vision for the flourishing of our city and we are simply following in their footsteps, seeking to fulfil our purpose in our generation – from generation, to generation, to generation.

Chapter Twenty-five
HOPE FOR THE CITY

Southampton's Bargate stands as one of the most iconic and enduring landmarks in the city. Steeped in more than 800 years of history, the Bargate was originally constructed during the Norman period, around 1180, serving as the primary entrance to the medieval walled city.

During the medieval period, the structure was enhanced with battlements and intricate stonework. Statues were added to honour key figures in the city's history, blending art and architecture in a way that celebrated Southampton's heritage.

Among the additions was the bell tower, situated at the south-west corner of the Bargate, added in 1605. The bell was used to signify curfews and sound alarms – a reminder of the ever-present need for vigilance in a time of political and military uncertainty. Yet this bell, centuries later, would come to symbolise something deeper than mere warnings; it would become a symbol of hope.

Bell of hope

During one of their regular prayer meetings, our prayer team embarked on a journey that led to the rediscovery of this ancient bell. As part of a broader exploration of Southampton's spiritual heritage, they were drawn to the bell tower in the Bargate. To their astonishment, they found that the bell had the word 'hope' inscribed on its surface.

Initially, we speculated that the bell might have been connected to the famous Isaac Watts hymn, 'O God, Our Help in Ages Past'. Watts, the prolific hymn writer, was born in Southampton in 1674 and remains one of the most influential voices in Christian hymnody. However, as we researched further, we realised that the bell itself predated Isaac Watts by several decades, ruling out any direct connection to his works.

Undeterred, we reached out to the City Council for further clarity, but no official records shed light on the origins of the inscription. While we may never know exactly why the word 'hope' was chosen, we were convinced that it was providential. In a world that often feels devoid of hope, the very existence of such an inscription felt like a message from the past to the present – a call to declare hope over our city.

Inspired by this discovery, we sought permission from the City Council to visit the bell tower, ring the bell, and symbolically declare hope over Southampton. Much to our delight, the council officers agreed. And so, on one brisk autumn morning, our small prayer team ascended the ancient stairs of the Bargate, made their way to the bell tower, and – after what we believe to be years of silence – rang out hope over the city.

For us, this was far more than a symbolic gesture. It was an act of faith and declaration that the future of Southampton could be filled with hope and possibility. In a time of uncertainty, economic challenges and social transformation, we wanted to proclaim that hope still had a place in the hearts and minds of our community. As the sound of the bell resonated through the streets below, we prayed for restoration, renewal and the uplifting of all who lived in the city.

The journey with Oasis academies

It was now 2014, and I had just stepped down as chair of the governing body for the Oasis academies. The years leading up to that moment had been both challenging and fulfilling. The task at hand had been significant: merging two schools on the west side of the city and two more on the east side into two brand-new, purpose-built facilities. These institutions, Oasis Academy Mayfield and Oasis Academy Lordshill, now served as beacons of hope and progress, offering high-quality education to hundreds of young people in Southampton.

This journey was anything but smooth. At the heart of it was the challenge of creating a distinctly Christ-centred organisation that could also embrace and celebrate the diversity of its students and staff. Oasis academies, with their vision rooted in the teachings of Jesus, aspired to be institutions that were welcoming to all, regardless of faith, background, or socioeconomic status. We understood that our calling was to recognise the inherent worth in every individual, just as Jesus did, and to create a learning environment that nurtured not just academic growth, but personal and spiritual development.

To guide this cultural transformation, the leadership team at Oasis developed a framework of nine habits – values that were promoted across all their activities and embedded in the everyday life of the academies. These nine habits were inspired by the life and teachings of Jesus: compassion, patience, humility, joy, honesty, hope, consideration, forgiveness and self-control. These habits weren't just abstract principles but lived values that we sought to instil in our students, staff and wider community.

The nine habits formed the foundation of the schools' ethos. From how students interacted with one another, to how teachers approached discipline and mentorship, these principles were constantly present. We wanted to create not only academically successful students but also compassionate, resilient and hopeful individuals who could navigate the complexities of modern life with grace and strength.

The impact was clear. More than 1,200 young people pass through the doors of Southampton Oasis academies each year, equipped not just with academic skills but with a deeper understanding of what it means to live in community with others. As a team, we knew that this investment in the next generation would bear fruit for years to come, as these students would go on to serve their communities with the same compassion and integrity that had been modelled for them.

Hope Community School

Just as my time with Oasis academies came to an end, a new challenge and opportunity emerged. In 2015, the Southampton City Council conducted a comprehensive review of primary school education in the city, and its findings were concerning: there would be a significant shortage of primary school places, particularly in the city centre, between 2015 and 2020. The solution was clear: the city needed new schools, and fast.

However, the only viable option for a brand-new school was through the government's Free School policy, which was part of the Conservative government's educational reforms. Free Schools were a new breed of institution, akin to the academies established under the previous Labour government, but with a stronger focus on community and parent-led initiatives. It was a system designed to allow local groups – whether charities, churches or parent organisations – to take the lead in establishing schools that would serve their specific communities.

At that point, my co-conspirator, Paul Woodman, approached me with a challenge: to do something about this shortage and spearhead the establishment of a new Free School in the city centre. The idea was daunting, but also deeply compelling. Southampton needed a new school, and with our experience in education and community engagement, we were uniquely positioned to meet that need.

Initially, I reached out to Oasis Community Learning to explore the possibility of partnering with them on this new venture. However, Oasis, already stretched with their existing commitments, did not have the capacity to take on another school at that time. It was then that I remembered hearing about the New Generation Schools Trust, a charity based in Sidcup, south-west London, that had already established a successful Free School there. We approached Paul Weston, the chair of the Trust, and he enthusiastically agreed to partner with us in creating a Free School for Southampton – a school we would name Hope Community School.

Building a school

The hard work began almost immediately. The New Generation Schools Trust took charge of developing the educational, financial and structural elements of the bid. Meanwhile, we had to conduct public consultations, engage with local parents, and convince them that this new school was not only necessary but also an ideal environment for their children.

Adam Clewer, our Next Generation leader, and Claire Rodgers, a member of our church with great local connections, formed a formidable team. Day after day, they canvassed local parks, knocked on doors, and organised public meetings, all in a bid to gather support from local parents. Their work paid off; by the time we presented our case to the Department for Education's commissioning team, we had strong community backing. The decision came through – the bid was successful, and Hope Community School was scheduled to open its doors in September 2016.

However, the journey was far from over. Finding a suitable venue for the school proved to be another major hurdle. We needed both temporary accommodation for the first few years of operation and a permanent site for the long-term.

One of the boldest and most exciting proposals we considered was using Central Hall as the permanent site for the new school. Central Hall, with its rich history and central location, seemed like a fitting home for an educational institution that was to embody hope and community. The trustees, enthusiastic yet pragmatic, formed a working group to explore the viability of this option. We held numerous discussions, conducted in-depth studies, and sought advice from architectural and educational experts. However, after several months of meetings and deliberations, it became clear that neither we nor the Department for Education (DfE) felt this was the most suitable long-term solution. It was disappointing, but we pressed on, undeterred.

While the vision of a permanent home was delayed, the search for temporary accommodation proved equally challenging. After weeks of exploring various avenues and facing one setback after another, the DfE team revisited the idea of using Central Hall as an interim location. Although this had not been our original plan, the more we discussed it, the more sense it seemed to make. Central Hall was already a hub for community activities, and the prospect of it temporarily hosting the new Hope Community School grew more appealing.

Once again, we entered detailed negotiations with the DfE. These were not easy discussions, but after months of back-and-forth deliberation, both sides reached a consensus. We agreed that Hope Community School would be housed at Central Hall for the first few years. As the partner church, we took on additional responsibilities, such as providing governance, chaplaincy and wrap-around services to support the wider school community. It was an exciting step forward, and we felt a strong sense of purpose in bringing education, hope and faith under one roof.

However, due to the delays in securing the venue, we had no choice but to postpone the school's opening to September 2017. This posed significant challenges. By that point, we had successfully recruited thirty children who were eager to begin their Reception year in September 2016. For the parents, the news of the delay was understandably disheartening, as it meant reshuffling their plans. For our team, it was an even more daunting task as we now had to recruit a new intake of children for the following year, all while retaining the confidence of the original families.

Though the postponement was a setback, it gave us the gift of time – time that proved invaluable. During this extra year, we managed to recruit an outstanding individual to lead the school. Steve Wright, a former student from the University of Southampton with deep ties to the church and the city, was appointed as the new headteacher. His background as an assistant headteacher in a London school, combined with his understanding of Southampton's unique community, made him an ideal fit for the role.

Securing Steve was a victory, and there was more good news to come. We finally identified a site for the new school, and architect's plans were drawn up. These were a tremendous asset in our efforts to recruit the next intake of students for 2017. Prospective parents could now see tangible evidence of the future we were building for their children.

A new role for Central Hall

The decision to house Hope Community School within Central Hall had a profound impact on both the church and the local community. On a practical level, the DfE's rental payments for the space covered all our utility and maintenance costs, relieving significant financial pressure. But the benefits went far beyond the financial. Up to this point, Central Hall, though physically located in the heart of the city, had been more of a Sunday morning destination for its congregation, most of whom drove in from other areas. The addition of the school fundamentally changed this dynamic. Central Hall was no longer just a place of worship; it was now a vibrant community hub, teeming with life and activity throughout the week, which was in line with the original Methodist vision that 'the Central Hall would be a busy hive of positive ideals with Christ at the centre'.

As we became more immersed in the community, we began to better understand its needs. One striking discovery was that 49 per cent of the children attending Hope Community School spoke English as an additional language. This presented both a challenge and an opportunity. Recognising the importance of supporting these families, we launched a Creative English programme, specifically designed to help parents improve their language skills. Annabel Wright, Steve's wife, was brought onto the team as a chaplain, working closely with families across the school community. Claire Rodgers, who had been a key figure in the project from the very beginning, became our dedicated parent liaison officer. Together, this team worked tirelessly to ensure that every family felt supported and welcomed.

Despite the progress, there were still obstacles to overcome. Planning permission for the new school site was ultimately refused due to concerns about flood risks. It was a significant blow, and once again, we found ourselves searching for a suitable location. Yet in the face of adversity, we chose to trust in a higher plan. As a team, we prayed earnestly for God to provide us with the land we needed – specifically, the plot opposite Central Hall, where the East Street Shopping Centre had once stood. The shopping centre had been demolished, and initial plans had been approved for a new supermarket. However, the supermarket chain decided to abandon their plans and sell the site.

The plot was then purchased by a hotel chain, which sought approval to build a large, multi-storey hotel. Throughout this time, we remained steadfast in our prayers, asking God to intervene and give us the land. Months passed without any activity on the site, and we grew increasingly curious. After a great deal of effort, we finally identified the owner and contacted his agent in Southampton. Our local city councillor, Darren Paffey, played an instrumental role in facilitating a meeting with the agent, which proved to be highly productive. The agent indicated that if the Department for Education could match the asking price, the owner would consider selling the land. After several more rounds of negotiation, the Department for Education's agents successfully reached an agreement. At long last, the deal was struck. We now had the land we had prayed for, but it would still be a few more years before the new school building would become a reality.

Building Hope, one class at a time

As of the time of writing, Hope Community School continues to operate out of Central Hall. The school has grown steadily, now boasting seven full classes and educating more than 200 young people. Our church remains actively involved at the governance level, ensuring that the school's foundational values of hope, faith and community are upheld. Steve Wright continues to serve as headteacher, and under his leadership, a dedicated team of teachers and support staff work tirelessly to bring hope and opportunity to hundreds of families in the city centre.

The end of an era and new beginnings

As the decade ended, we witnessed several changes and developments across the church. Sim Dendy accepted an invitation to become senior leader at New Life Church in Romsey, marking a new chapter in his journey. Meanwhile, Theo and Sarah Amer took on leadership roles at Central Hall, overseeing the congregational team. Mikey Powell, a talented musician and songwriter with a rich Christian heritage, was employed as the worship director, bringing fresh energy and creativity to our gatherings.

Other members of our church family were also embarking on new adventures. Adam Clewer, his American wife, Sarah, and their family relocated to the USA, where Adam assumed the role of senior pastor at a church near Boston. Similarly, Mark and Mel Simpson, and Carl and Mel Wills, moved on to new horizons. The Simpsons returned to their beloved South Africa, while Carl Wills ventured into the business world, starting a company with his brother. Steve Lee moved his Miracle Street evangelistic ministry base to a church in Winchester. The ministry was now taking all his time as he served and supported churches in their outreach.

Amid these changes, we had the privilege of being featured once again on the BBC, this time for a live, hour-long service on Pentecost Sunday. The service was a powerful reminder of the reach and impact of our church community. During this period, the Flowers congregation merged with City Life Church, a decision that made practical sense as both groups were meeting in the same building. This merger freed Bob Light to focus on his pastoral work, serving the people on the local housing estate with renewed vigour.

Our work at the Orchard Lane Church came to an end. The building was taken over by friends and church members David and Anna Wright, owners of Paint Pots nurseries, who opened a pre-school nursery in the building that would serve as a feeder nursery for Hope Community School.

While our efforts at home were flourishing, we also felt a calling to extend our mission overseas. After much prayer and discernment, we launched a new initiative called New Community Kibera, focused on serving one of the largest slums in Africa, located in Nairobi, Kenya. This mission was a bold step of faith, born out of a desire to bring life to some of the most vulnerable communities in the world. Dave Boniface took on the task of building a team to form partnerships with local people developing small businesses, providing community health education and facilitating the setting up of a football academy.

Back in Europe, we made the difficult decision to sell our property in Normandy, France. Michael and Amanda Thom had been exemplary hosts, but the financial strain of maintaining the property was no longer sustainable. Around the same time, we released our Eastleigh congregation, allowing them to form their own independent church and charity, which they named Thrive Church.

Preparing for the future

In anticipation of Hope Community School eventually moving into its permanent facility, we established a new trading company, New Community Ventures. This company was tasked with managing Central Hall and developing alternative income streams to ensure the long-term sustainability of the building. We knew that when the time came for the school to relocate, Central Hall would once again become a central hub for the community, and we were determined to ensure it would thrive for generations to come.

The school and trading initiatives reflected the richness of God's blessing on us. As the school's name proclaimed, God's people were able to declare hope and salvation to a city, reaching the influential, touching the lost and destitute and proclaiming blessing to the city.

Chapter Twenty-six

SEASONS OF FRUITFULNESS

In the latter part of 2019, I found myself standing in the familiar space of Central Hall, preaching to a congregation I had come to know and love over many years. It was a typical Sunday, yet something significant stirred within me, something I hadn't fully expected. As I spoke, a deep sense of prophetic *unction* came over me, a feeling that transcended the ordinary flow of the sermon. My heart was drawn to a particular passage in the Gospel of John, one that I had read and preached on many times before, but today, it resonated with new urgency. The words of Jesus echoed in my spirit:

> If you remain in me and my words remain in you, ask whatever you wish, and it will be done for you. This is to my Father's glory, that you bear much fruit, showing yourselves to be my disciples.
>
> (John 15:7-8)

Call to action

As I stood before the congregation, I knew these words were not just for the moment but carried a weight for the season we were entering, a season of fruitfulness. I began speaking directly to those who had been with the church through the years – many who had been there from the very beginning, faithfully remaining, even when others had come and gone. There was a special sense that those who had remained, those who had endured the journey, were now entering into a place where they would experience much answered prayer, where their faithfulness would be met with divine favour. And so, with a boldness that surprised even me, I declared to the congregation:

> For those of you who have remained, when others have come and gone, know that the Father is waiting to hear your prayers. His ears are attentive to the prayers of those who have remained steadfast. Whatever you ask will be done for you, because you have been tested, refined and your hearts are pure.

I continued, sensing this was a message that needed to be spoken over those present:

> This is a season where, through your prayers, you will see many of the things you have longed for, come to pass. In fact, you will witness more fruitfulness in this season through your prayers than in all the years of your activity.

The response was immediate and deeply encouraging. People received the word with open hearts, and it became clear that this was not just a message for that Sunday morning, but a call to action. We quickly decided to gather those who felt particularly aligned with this message – the ones who had 'remained' – and form a prayer group. This group would focus on intercession for the church, its mission and the leadership. And so, on a cold Monday morning in January 2020, the first 'Remainers prayer meeting' was held at Central Hall. Despite the chill in the air, the gathering was marked by a powerful time of worship and deep intercession. Week by week, momentum grew as we came together to pray, united by a shared sense of purpose.

One of the early prayer focuses during these meetings was the future of the church's leadership. For some time, I had been sensing that my season as senior leader was nearing its end. Over the past decade, I had taken on multiple roles, leading the local church while also heading up the Pioneer network of churches, serving as one of the presidents of Churches Together in England, and working as an ecumenical canon at Winchester Cathedral. Additionally, I had been helping to develop the international arm of Pioneer, which demanded more of my attention. While I had dedicated myself to resetting the church's vision and building partnerships across the city, I knew the time was approaching for someone else to step into the role, someone who could devote themselves fully to New Community Church and its mission in Southampton. The church needed a leader whose heart and energy would be focused on guiding it into its next season of life and growth.

Lockdown

But before we could take any steps towards this leadership transition, the world changed in an instant. Early in March 2020, we watched with growing concern as the COVID-19 pandemic swept across Europe. The virus spread rapidly, devastating hospitals in Italy and Spain, and it soon became clear that the United Kingdom would not be spared. By mid-March, the number of cases in the UK was rising sharply, and the government responded with increasing urgency. Initial recommendations of social distancing and self-isolation quickly gave way to stricter measures, and on 23rd March, Prime Minister Boris Johnson announced a full national lockdown.

The lockdown had an immediate and profound impact on our church. Almost overnight, we were forced to suspend all public worship gatherings, closing the doors of Central Hall to the congregation for the first time in living memory. Hope Community School, which operated within our building, remained open with limited attendance, though under stringent social distancing protocols. The rapid pace of these changes required us to act quickly. In the days leading up to the lockdown, our leadership team worked tirelessly to develop a strategy for navigating this unprecedented situation.

Our first priority was to ensure that the most vulnerable within our community were cared for. We established a dedicated email address for those needing extra support or for those able to offer assistance. Additionally, we mobilised our small group leaders to create a 'buddy' system, ensuring that no one fell through the cracks during this isolating time. We were determined that everyone in our community, regardless of age or circumstance, would feel connected and supported.

Good communication was essential, so we set up dedicated Facebook groups for each of our congregations, as well as for Hope Community School and those involved in our Community Hub activities. These platforms allowed us to maintain a sense of connection even when physical meetings were impossible. We also transitioned quickly to livestreaming our services. Initially, these streams were filmed in an empty Central Hall, an experience that was surreal for both those of us leading and those watching from home. However, as the weeks progressed, we shifted to streaming from our homes, aiming to create a more personal and intimate atmosphere. Theo and Sarah Amer anchored the Central Hall congregation's livestream, while Clive and Jane Wiseman did the same for the congregation meeting at St Andrew's Methodist Church in Sholing. Each team, supported by our dedicated technical crew, did an extraordinary job of providing stability and comfort in what was an incredibly disorientating time. The worship team also adapted to the new normal, recording worship sessions that were 'almost live' and maintaining a sense of the communal worship experience we all missed.

The adjustment to online church life was rapid, but not without its challenges. We learned how to record and upload talks to our YouTube channel, and Zoom became the primary platform for most of our midweek meetings, including the newly formed Remainers Prayer Group.

Despite the initial awkwardness of moving to virtual meetings, there was a surprising sense of excitement about how this season might reshape the church. We began to sense that God was at work, even in the midst of such uncertainty and disruption. In the book of Acts, we read about how the persecution of the early Church in Jerusalem scattered believers throughout Judea and Samaria. As they went, they preached the word wherever they found themselves. Similarly, the pandemic had thrust us into a situation we hadn't planned for, but we believed that God would use this time to multiply the work of the church and accelerate our journey towards a fuller expression of his vision for Southampton.

And beyond

Just as the early apostles had to trust the Spirit in the face of uncertainty, we too had to lean into faith, believing that God was orchestrating something beyond our immediate understanding. The lockdowns, though difficult, gave us the opportunity to step back and reflect on the future. A small group of leaders, which included several of our trustees and members of the leadership team, began meeting regularly to consider how the church might emerge from the pandemic. We called this group the Task and Finish Group, and its purpose was to clarify our vision for the post-lockdown world. Over many months of often intense and, at times, tumultuous conversations, we arrived at a shared understanding of where God was leading us.

We clarified our vision as a church – to see the whole church, following the way of Jesus, making disciples and bringing life and transformation to every area of Southampton and beyond. It was a vision rooted in our belief that changed lives would lead to transformed communities. Our mission, in essence, was to be agents of that transformation, bringing the life and hope of Jesus to every corner of our city. We spent significant time thinking through how we might achieve this vision. Our strategy would focus on cultivating a culture of deep devotion and dependence on Jesus, empowering and releasing every member of the church to be a bringer of life to their communities, and serving the most vulnerable. We also recognised that we had a role to play in the long-term spiritual, social and cultural renewal of Southampton.

To make this vision a reality, we knew we needed to align our leadership structure with our mission. It was at this point that I felt a strong conviction that I needed to step aside and allow new leadership to take the church forward. I had pondered it for a while, but now, I felt, it was time. The church was in a pivotal season, and I believed it was time for a new generation of leaders to take the reins, leading the church with fresh energy and focus into the next chapter of its story.

Theo and Sarah

We began a process of discernment to determine who should lead New Community Church into this new season. A small group was formed to guide this process, consisting of the chair of trustees, two members of the existing leadership, and Richard Anniss from the Pioneer National Leadership Team. It quickly became apparent that Theo and Sarah Amer were the natural choice for this role. Having been part of the leadership team for more than two decades, they were deeply respected within the congregation and across the wider Church community in Southampton. Since 2018, they had been leading the Central Hall congregation and, during the pandemic, they had been the steady, reassuring presence that many in the church needed.

Theo had moved to Southampton in the mid-1990s to attend university, but his journey towards leadership had begun long before. Raised in Exeter, Theo's family was deeply rooted in one of the early charismatic and house church networks led by Pastor Wally North. This influential Bradford-based movement had merged with Bryn Jones' Harvestime network in the 1970s. Growing up in this environment, Theo's leadership qualities were naturally nurtured. He absorbed the values of servanthood, spiritual leadership and community building, and it became increasingly clear to those around him that his path was one of church leadership. His ability to unite people, cast vision and guide others through challenges was undeniable, reflecting the foundational principles he had inherited from his family's deep spiritual heritage.

Sarah, meanwhile, had a distinct but equally powerful journey. Her home church was Arun Community Church in Littlehampton, home of the Delirious? band. From a young age, Sarah was surrounded by a culture of passionate worship and vibrant faith, and she was heavily involved with the original Cutting Edge events in her hometown. When she moved to Southampton to study in the mid-1990s, she brought with her a strong gift of worship and a deep prophetic calling. She immediately integrated into the local church's worship team, where her resilient faith became evident. No matter the season or challenge, Sarah's unwavering trust in God, combined with her prophetic insight, became a source of strength for the church community. Her gift for worship was not merely about leading songs but about creating an atmosphere where people could encounter God in powerful and transformative ways.

In the early 2000s, Theo and Sarah had experienced a profound season of deep challenge that tested their faith and resilience. Their journey began with the premature birth of their first child, a moment that brought both joy and fear. The uncertainty of a fragile newborn added immense pressure, yet it was during this time that Theo's clear leadership calling began to emerge. He found strength in the midst of chaos, providing support and guidance not only for Sarah, but also for their family and the church community around them.

As they navigated the complexities of parenthood, they faced additional heartache through a series of miscarriages. Each loss was a heavy burden, yet Sarah's unwavering faith became a beacon of hope for those around her. She clung to God's promises, demonstrating a resilience that inspired others. Her ability to lean on her faith, even in the face of repeated loss, reflected her deep-rooted trust in God's plan.

Through their trials, Theo and Sarah consistently sought God's guidance and comfort. They prayed earnestly and held onto the belief that God had a purpose for their lives and family. It was this unwavering trust that ultimately sustained them, leading to the joyful arrival of their second daughter. The journey they walked together solidified their bond and deepened their commitment to one another and their faith. They emerged from this season not just as a couple but as a testament to the power of resilience and trust in God amid adversity.

Their experience not only shaped their own lives, but also became a source of encouragement for others facing similar challenges, demonstrating that faith can thrive even in the darkest moments.

The discernment process, while thorough, confirmed what many of us already knew – Theo and Sarah were called to lead the church in the years to come. With a clear sense of calling and commitment to the vision, Theo and Sarah officially began their transition into the role of senior leaders in the summer of 2022. Although the transition was announced publicly at that time, the process had begun months earlier as we navigated the changes necessitated by the pandemic.

Commissioning

By 1st September 2022, the leadership mantle had fully passed from Caroline and me to Theo and Sarah. The formal celebration and commissioning took place at Central Hall over a weekend in early October. The weekend was filled with joy, reflection and gratitude for all that God had done over the past two decades.

On the Saturday, friends, family and city church leaders gathered with current and former church members for a wonderful buffet meal in the main hall. Images from our leadership over the years were being shown on the screen. I did remark that felt a little like attending your own funeral!

Theo and Sarah hosted the evening and there were heartfelt speeches from friends and congregation members, our soon-to-be Member of Parliament, and the former Bishop of Southampton who spoke with warmth and wisdom, bringing a sense of history and continuity to the moment.

It was a fun evening with lots of kind words and gifts showered on Caroline and me.

The next morning, Ness Wilson, who leads the Pioneer network in the UK, preached the commissioning sermon. Her words were both profound and uplifting as we marked the passing of responsibility to Theo and Sarah. We were passing a torch, fired by the hopes and prayers of generations before them, and urged the congregation to reflect not only on the past, but also on the bright and promising future that lay ahead.

It was especially poignant that Hannah Strutt, formerly Morton, attended the commissioning. She had been the one alongside Tony who had prayed for and commissioned Caroline and me twenty years before. At that event in January 2002, Hannah had presented Caroline with an ornate antique key as a symbol of the responsibility and authority that Caroline now had as leader of the church. Caroline had kept the key in safekeeping for all these years. On a visit to a church leaders' conference a few years before, she had found a painting of the exact key and the title for the painting was *Revelation*.[10] On that Sunday Caroline, supported by Hannah, presented Sarah with the key and the painting.

As Caroline passed the key to Sarah that day, she spoke words that carried the weight of two decades of leadership and prayer:

> When we were prayed into leadership, the words spoken over us were 'Generations, Generations, Generations'. That word has shaped our time here, watching the passing of the baton from one generation to another. But for you, Sarah, the word is different. For you, the word is 'Revelation, Revelation, Revelation'. Your leadership will be marked by hearing and discerning God's voice for each step you take. Just as we have seen God's faithfulness over these years, we are confident that he will continue to guide you as you listen for his voice and lead this church into the next season.

As the key passed from one hand to another, from one generation to the next, there was a palpable sense that something significant was taking place. This was not just a symbolic gesture, but the beginning of a new chapter for the church, one where a new generation of leaders would step into their calling, supported by the faithful prayers of those who had remained.

The transition was not only a passing of responsibility, but a moment that encapsulated the heart of what it means to follow Jesus. It was a reminder that leadership in the kingdom of God is not about holding onto power or position, but about faithful stewardship, about nurturing what God has entrusted to us and then passing it on to the next generation when the time comes. And so, with hearts full of gratitude and expectation, we handed over the leadership of New Community Church, confident that the future was in good hands and that God would continue to do 'immeasurably more' than we could ask or imagine in the years to come (Ephesians 3:20).

Chapter Twenty-seven

Fifty Years and Counting

As we approach the remarkable milestone of our fiftieth anniversary as a church, we take this opportunity to reflect on our journey with deep gratitude, recognising that by God's enduring grace, we stand today in a place of health and strength.

Here we stand

The first and most significant reason to celebrate is, quite simply, that we are still here. In an era where many church communities have faltered, our continued presence is no small feat.

Roger Forster, former leader of the Ichthus Christian Fellowship, authored a book in 1986 titled *Ten New Churches*,[11] which documented the journeys of ten churches birthed during the charismatic and new church movements of the 1970s. Of those ten, only four still exist today, and even they bear little resemblance to their former selves. This sobering reality highlights the inherent fragility of church movements, and underscores how profoundly blessed we are to have weathered the storms of the past five decades – steadfast and resilient in the face of trials.

Many churches crumble under the weight of leadership failures, or struggle to remain relevant in an ever-evolving society. Yet, here we stand, a testament to God's unyielding faithfulness and the resilience he has instilled within our congregation. We have faced numerous challenges, but through it all, God has been our guiding light, leading us through each trial and helping us to navigate our way forward.

It's true that the number of people attending our Sunday services has declined from the heights we reached in 2002/03. Up to that time, we were among the few charismatic churches in the city, drawing in people who were hungry for Spirit-led worship, solid biblical teaching, and a vibrant, close-knit community. But today, the spiritual landscape has expanded. Many more dynamic churches now offer what was once unique to us, giving people a broader array of opportunities to grow in their faith.

Moreover, we've seen members move on for various reasons: some to support smaller local churches, others drawn to a more traditional style of worship, and still others who, while maintaining their personal faith, have chosen to disengage from the formal structures of 'organised religion'. Some have wrestled with reconciling long-held traditional beliefs – particularly on issues like human sexuality – with contemporary perspectives, leading them to step away. And, of course, there are those who have lost their faith entirely.

However, we have come to recognise that Sunday attendance alone is no longer the definitive measure of success. While numbers and tithe income are quantifiable markers, they do not capture the full breadth of a church's reach and influence. The true impact of our community stretches far beyond our services and gatherings, touching countless lives through a diverse range of ministries. From Hope Community School to our Warm Spaces project and the Community Hub activities at Central Hall, serving the families at the school and in the SO14 area, the Community Café, and our recently formed partnership with the charity Hope Into Action and the houses they facilitate for the homeless, our mission is alive and thriving in numerous tangible ways. The Sholing congregation with their regular community activities and the New Community Kibera team are continuing to extend the church's mission locally and globally.

When we take a broader view, the influence of our community over five decades becomes even more striking. Consider the 45,000 patients now served by the General Practice partnership that was birthed from the vision of two young doctors in the early 1980s. Or the thousands of young people who have passed through The King's School and the Oasis academies, receiving not just a quality education, but an understanding of Jesus' teachings. Families have been profoundly enriched through David and Anna Wright's Paint Pots nurseries, while scores of men and women have found support through Groundswell, the Crossroads helpline, the Firgrove Family Trust, Central Counselling and Training Service and the Southampton Family Trust.

And the reach of our mission extends even further. We have baptised hundreds of people. Countless individuals have experienced life-changing encounters with God through the ministry of the church and the churches we've planted across the city and beyond, the outreach programmes we've organised and the events we've hosted.

Internationally, through the work of the School of Ministries, we've trained tens of thousands of leaders, and in partnership with c.net and Pioneer we have supported fledgling churches in some of the world's most challenging environments and raised substantial funds to uplift the most vulnerable.

Equally importantly, we've come to deeply value the everyday contributions of our congregation members in their respective fields. Whether business leaders, doctors, nurses, social workers, teachers or caregivers, our community serves the city in transformative ways. Many volunteer as school governors, celebrants, magistrates, city guides and charity workers. Each person increasingly embraces their unique role, recognising that they are part of a broader mission to bring God's love and transformation to the city.

If someone had told that small, ragtag group of fifty mostly young people gathered on Sunday, 2nd March 1975, what would unfold over the next fifty years, they would scarcely have believed it.

Today

Caroline and I are still very much part of the church community serving in various capacities; Caroline regularly offering healing prayer while I continue to chair the Hope Community School governing board. We are still operating as leaders of the Pioneer International network, which involves us travelling extensively throughout the year.

Caroline's diagnosis with breast cancer in late 2020 and subsequent chemotherapy treatment has made us value the importance of each day that we have, and the importance of the people and relationships that God has placed in our lives. We are thrilled to have been able to play our part in the journey of the church; to have fulfilled our assignment and to have handed over responsibility to the next generation.

Theo and Sarah, along with an excellent leadership team – including Clive and Jane Wiseman from Sholing, Mikey Powell as head of Devotion and Worship, Esther Manners leading Pastoral Care and Flora Hinks overseeing Mission and Discipleship – have built upon the church's foundational values, setting a clear vision for the future. Together, they've refined a set of core values, which have been present since the church's early days but are now expressed with greater clarity:

Presence

We prioritise God's presence in everything we do. Whether individually or when we gather, we invite the Holy Spirit to lead us and let Scripture guide our steps. We believe we are created for union with Jesus, who is always with us. Our awareness of his presence is what shapes us into the people and community God intended us to be.

Growth

We equip and empower each other to grow in faith, character, and gifting. Our goal is to become mature followers of Christ, rooted in faith and humility. Growth, both personal and communal, leads to fruitfulness, and we invest in helping one another develop spiritually.

Community

We foster environments where relationships can flourish. We were made to live in community, both with God and each other. As a church, we are devoted to loving one another, honouring each other, rejoicing together in good times, mourning together in hardship, and joyfully serving the Lord in unity. We strive to create spaces where everyone feels they belong.

Ownership

We all play a part in God's vision for this community. Each of us has a role to fulfil, and we serve with initiative and excellence, asking ourselves, 'What can I do to help this community thrive?' We take ownership of the church's mission, choosing to contribute our best.

Confidence

The gospel of Jesus Christ is central to everything we do. It brings salvation, redemption and restoration to all who believe. Having discovered the joy of knowing Christ, we share this good news with confidence, trusting in its power to transform lives. We seek opportunities for others to encounter Jesus and experience the same joy.

Outward-looking

We extend love and hospitality beyond the church walls. Whether within our church family, in our neighbourhoods, workplaces or communities, we serve with Christ-like love, always responsive to the needs around us. We seek to embody the gospel through both words and actions, welcoming the stranger and serving those in need with open hearts.

There is also a strong team in place, supporting the church's various operations. From administration to finance, from children and youth work to student outreach, these dedicated individuals ensure the day-to-day functions of the church run smoothly. Our trustees continue to offer vital support, advice and expertise, while the New Community Ventures team, now six members strong, is committed to maintaining Central Hall and securing its financial sustainability.

The mission of the church is alive and thriving, with Hubs – mid-sized groups designed to live out the vision and values of New Community Church – at the forefront. A new discipleship pathway has been established, providing clear steps for those seeking to grow in their faith.

There has been a necessary and renewed emphasis on evangelism. Alpha courses have been revived with fresh enthusiasm under new leadership, and baptisms are taking place regularly, signalling the continued growth of our community. The work among young people and students is expanding, laying the groundwork for the next generation of believers.

As we celebrate fifty years, we give thanks for all that God has done, is doing and will continue to do in and through our church. We remain confident that the best is yet to come.

Final reflections

We were birthed in a season of renewal, a time when our hearts and spirits were reawakened by the Holy Spirit to the vibrant life and joy that comes with salvation in Christ. It was a period of discovery, where we encountered the deep, transformative power of God's presence and realised our lives were woven into his eternal story.

The teachings of men like Arthur Wallis, Ern Baxter and Bryn Jones profoundly shaped us. Their passion for revival and the vision for a church restored to New Testament ideals captured our hearts. They called us to awaken to the reality of God's kingdom on earth now, to live not just for ourselves but for a greater purpose – participating in God's ongoing work of redemption and renewal.

We modelled a new way of being church. We broke out of restrictive traditions. We tried things for the first time. Sometimes we were successful, at other times we had to pull back and try something different. We weren't afraid to fail because our overriding commitment to God's purpose and mission was unwavering.

We learned to live by radical faith. Trusting God was no longer just a concept but the very fabric of our existence. In small moments and bold leaps of faith, we relied on him completely. We made big decisions, stepped into the unknown, confident that God would guide, provide and sustain us. We learned to listen to his voice, respond to the prophetic word and rely on him.

Along the way, we found friends who shared our passion for the church and the longing for revival. Some of these friendships became lifelong companions on the journey, relationships forged in the fires of faith and tested through life's trials. Together, we laughed, cried and grew, journeying deeper into the heart of God. Other friends joined us on the journey for a season. They made their contribution, added who they were to us and moved on.

We found a home in a community of faith, a place where we could be vulnerable, grow and find strength. Church moved from being a Sunday-centric activity to a 24/7 community where our faith was nurtured, and where we experienced the power of unity and love firsthand.

Within this community of faith, we not only found belonging, but a sense of purpose. As we grew in understanding God's heart, we all discovered our unique place in his story. We grew in our awareness that we weren't called to live ordinary lives, but to be part of something far greater – a movement of God's Spirit in our time.

We learned to love our city and, more importantly, its people. No longer did we see them as projects to be managed, problems to be solved, or even as disembodied souls waiting to be saved. We came to view each person as a unique individual, deeply loved by God and valuable to him.

This shift transformed our approach to ministry. We understood that our mission wasn't about quick fixes or one-time interventions, but about walking alongside people, understanding their stories and supporting them in their journeys. Our focus expanded to create lasting change, addressing not just spiritual needs but physical, emotional and social ones as well.

Our thinking, our theology and our practices evolved over the years. We grew to love the whole Church, supporting and celebrating others as they pursued God and his mission. We realised we had much to learn from churches that had been around for many years more than us.

The journey, however, was not without its hardships. Alongside the joy and discovery, we experienced heartache, pain and loss. There were seasons of trial, times when the weight of the world pressed heavily upon us, and moments when the path forward seemed unclear. Sometimes in our zeal we made mistakes, people were hurt, and we had to apologise.

In these valleys of life, we came to know God's faithfulness not just as theory, but in the most tangible and personal ways. His presence became our constant companion, his promises our sure foundation. In every trial, he proved again and again that he was with us, never leaving or forsaking us, carrying us through every storm.

Standing in this moment, looking back at the road we've travelled, we realise that every challenge and triumph, every joy and sorrow, is a testimony of God's incredible faithfulness. We see the rich tapestry God has woven – threads of renewal, faith, community and unwavering love. Each moment, whether filled with joy or sorrow, has contributed to the masterpiece he's been crafting in our lives.

We haven't seen all that we longed for, had every prayer answered, or seen every prophetic word fulfilled, but we've learned to trust him more deeply, love him more passionately, and follow him more courageously.

Our journey is far from over.

When God breathed our church into existence, he saw something, he saw who we could become, and he continues to call us into that destiny.

There is still more that God has yet to do. Another generation now has the task to push forward, and we know that God's grace will sustain them, his love will guide them and his faithfulness will never fail them.

> Let this be written for a future generation,
> that a people not yet created may praise the Lord.
>
> (Psalm 102:18)

For Further Reading

Bruce Atkinson, *Land of Hope and Glory: British Revival Through the Ages* (London: Dovewell Publications, 2003)

A. John Carr, *The Emerging Church: In Ephesians* (Decatur, GA: Charis Publications, 1980)

Phillip Clarke, *A Heart of Compassion* (Milton Keynes: Authentic Media, 2006)

John Fleming, *Bind us Together* (Seaford: Thankful Books, 2007)

Roger Forster, ed., *Ten New Churches* (Bromley: MARC Europe, 1986)

Eddie Gibbs and Ryan Bolger, *Emerging Churches: Creating Christian Community in Postmodern Cultures* (Grand Rapids, MI: Baker Academic, 2005)

Brian Hewitt, *Doing a New Thing?: Seven Leaders Reflect on the Past, Present and Future of the House Church Movement* (London: Hodder & Stoughton, 1995)

Peter Hocken, *Streams of Renewal* (Milton Keynes: Paternoster Press, 1986)

Peter Hocken, *The Glory and the Shame* (Guildford: Eagle, 1994)

William K. Kay, *Apostolic Networks in Britain: New Ways of Being Church* (Milton Keynes: Paternoster, 2007)

Bob Light, *This is My Offering* (self-published, 2018)

David Lillie, *Restoration: Is This Still On God's Programme* (self-published, 1994)

John McKay, *Movements of the Spirit: A History of the Prophetic Church* (Norwich: The Way of the Spirit, 2000)

Les Moir, *Missing Jewel: The Worship Movement that Impacted the Nations* (Colorado Springs: David Cook, 2017)

Watchman Nee, *The Normal Christian Life* (Eastbourne: Victory Press, 1957)

John Noble, *The Shaking* (Oxford: Monarch Books, 2002)

Juan Carlos Ortiz, *Disciple* (London: Lakeland Books, 1975)

Roy Pearson, *Divine Encounters* (self-published, 2021)

Nigel Scotland, *Charismatics and the Next Millennium* (London: Hodder & Stoughton, 1995)

Ralph Turner, *Gerald Coates Pioneer* (Welwyn Garden City: Malcolm Down Publishing, 2015)

Terry Virgo, *No Well-Worn Paths: Restoring the Church to Christ's Original Intention* (Eastbourne: Kingsway, 2001)

Terry Virgo, *Restoration in the Church* (Eastbourne: Kingsway, 1985)

Andrew Walker, *Restoring the Kingdom: The Radical Christianity of the House Church Movement* (Fully Revised and Expanded Edition) (Guildford: Eagle, 1998)

Jonathan Wallis, Arthur Wallis: *Radical Christian* (Eastbourne: Kingsway Publications, 1991)

Andrew Whitman, *When Jesus Met Hippies* (Welwyn Garden City: Malcolm Down Publishing, 2023)

Further Information

New Community Church Southampton:
https://newcommunity.org.uk/

Pioneer Network:
https://pioneer.org.uk/

Billy Kennedy is the leader of Pioneer International Network, an ecumenical canon at Winchester Cathedral and a former president of Churches Together in England. He serves as a visitor for the Order of the Mustard Seed ecumenical missional order and was the senior leader at New Community Church in Southampton from 2002-22. Billy is married to Caroline and they have three children, David, Erin and Daniel, and five grandchildren.

Ralph Turner is a Christian author specialising in biographies and ghostwritten autobiographies. He is based in Leicester, UK.

ralphturnerwriter.com

Endnotes

Chapter Two
1. R.A. Torrey, *The Baptism with the Holy Spirit* (Chicago, IL: Fleming H. Revell Company, 1895).

Chapter Three
2. Arthur Wallis, *In the Day of Thy Power* (London: CLC Publications, 1956).

Chapter Nine
3. Andrew Walker, *Restoring the Kingdom* (Guildford: Eagle Publishing, 1998).
4. Jonathan Wallis, *Arthur Wallis: Radical Christian* (Eastbourne: Kingsway Publications, 1991), pp. 309-310.

Chapter Twelve
5. Ralph Neighbour, *Where Do We Go from Here?* (Houston, TX: Touch Outreach Ministries, 2000).

Chapter Thirteen
6. Pete Greig, Dave Roberts, *Red Moon Rising* (Eastbourne: Kingsway Publications, 2004), pp.93-94.

Chapter Fourteen
7. www.youtube.com/watch?v=5bznSNJx3ns (accessed 7.1.25).

Chapter Sixteen
8. Suzanne Baker, Chris Davis, Christine Seed, *Saints of a Different League* (London: The Shaftsbury Society, 2006).

Chapter Twenty-four

9. Mark Stibbe and Andrew Williams, *Breakout* (Milton Keynes: Authentic, 2008).

Chapter Twenty-six

10. Unfound.

Chapter Twenty-seven

11. Roger Forster, *Ten New Churches* (Charlotte, NC: Christian Research, 1986).